D1717026

Floral Patterns For Stencilling

With Full Instructions for Wall Printing

Susan M. Britton &
Jackie N. Looney

Sterling Publishing Co., Inc.   New York

This book is dedicated to all those who have loved and supported me throughout the years.

—Jackie Looney

Library of Congress Cataloging-in-Publication Data
Britton, Susan M.
    Floral patterns for stencilling.
    Includes index.
    1. Stencils and stencil cutting.   2. Design,
Decorative—Plant forms.   I. Looney, Jackie N.
II. Title.
TT270.B85   1986   745.7'3   85-27718
ISBN 0-8069-4728-4
ISBN 0-8069-4730-6 (pbk.)

Copyright © 1986 by Susan M. Britton, artwork by Jackie N. Looney
Published by Sterling Publishing Co., Inc.
Two Park Avenue, New York, N.Y. 10016
Distributed in Australia by Capricorn Book Co. Pty. Ltd.
Unit 5C1 Lincoln St., Lane Cove, N.S.W. 2066
Distributed in the United Kingdom by Blandford Press
Link House, West Street, Poole, Dorset BH15 1LL, England
Distributed in Canada by Oak Tree Press Ltd.
℅ Canadian Manda Group. P.O. Box 920, Station U
Toronto, Ontario, Canada M8Z 5P9
Manufactured in the United States of America
All rights reserved

CONTENTS

Blackberries, page 41

Fuchsia, page 44

Fern, page 61

Calla Lily, page 69

4

Forget-Me-Not, page 82

Begonia, page 93

California Poppy, page 107

Nasturtium, page 118

Rose, page 129

6

Daffodil, page 141

MATERIALS AND TECHNIQUES

Imagine eating breakfast in a field of California poppies. Or playing Chopin on your grand piano in a garden of begonias. Or lying on your bed at night, encircled by fuchsia nodding gently in the moonlight.

These possibilities are yours, using the stencilled flower borders in this book, which were designed by California artist Jackie Looney.

Stencilling is an ancient art. In the Middle Ages, Europeans used it to illuminate manuscripts. In the Orient, some of the most delicate, complicated stencils ever made were used to decorate silks. Later, in colonial America, stencilling took the place of wallpaper, as itinerant stencillers covered whole walls with stylized pineapples and silhouettes of squirrels.

In recent times, prompted in part by the renovation of old houses, the stencil has experienced a revival. Unfortunately, the revival has been timid, and most designs available in kits and books are static images.

But Jackie Looney has expanded the technique to create flowing, energetic imagery as delicate as rose petals. She calls her craft *wall printing* to differentiate it from the common, static stencil.

This book illustrates ten designs—eight of flowers, one of ferns, and one of blackberry vines. In addition, there are three miniborders that can be used to edge the larger designs. The designs are intended as trimming for ceilings, floors, or wainscoting, just as rickrack might decorate the hem of a dress. They differ greatly in mood and style, from the loose, wild California poppy to the elegant rose.

Most of us think of stencils as images that are duplicated every few inches. But this is not the case in nature or in wall printing.

With one design—the wide fern border—individual fronds, curled and uncurled, can be printed at will and at random. Other designs include a "random element," that—like a sprig of foliage on a bouquet—can expand the design. Even when the borders are printed in the conventional, repeating manner, the design flows together so that it is difficult to tell where the image repeats itself.

Simple freehand techniques to shade and vein leaves add to the illusion that the flowery borders are the original artwork of a naturalist. And the freehand work is simple enough for anyone.

And anyone who can stencil can wall-print. The added requirements are time, patience, and know-how, not skill. Wall-printing is like knitting a sweater on small needles instead of giant ones: It may be more time-consuming, but it yields a finer, more delicate result.

How to Use This Book

Stencilling is a printing process. The design is cut into a stiff piece of paper or plastic called a template. The resulting holes in the template represent the design you want to appear on the wall. The template is held firmly to the wall to be printed. When paint is brushed over the template, it produces a design where the holes have been cut. In Jackie Looney's wall prints, several images are layered to form the design.

General instructions that apply to all the designs are given first. Also included are a materials list and methods for preparing the wall surface, sizing the stencil to the room, and cutting and printing. The designs themselves appear in the order of their difficulty of execution. Additional instructions are given with each design to help you cope with its peculiarities. Most of the borders look best printed on a stripe of color that contrasts with the wall. Otherwise, the stems will seem to float in space. Therefore, instructions for painting a stripe and for several miniborders, which can be used to finish off the look of a design, are also included.

The troubleshooting section (page 37) can help solve problems that may arise.

Materials

PAINT

Acrylics: Artists' acrylic paints (Illus. 1) are sold in small tubes in art-supply shops. Jackie prefers them to all others because of their brilliant, intense colors. They are water based, which means they can be thinned and cleaned with water, thus avoiding the inconvenience of using mineral spirits or turpentine, which are required with oil-based paint. They dry fast, enabling you to work without worrying about smearing what is already on the wall. The major problem with acrylics is that they lack opacity. But this can be overcome by mixing them with a few drops of flat white latex house paint. Jackie keeps a soap dish or shampoo bottle filled with white house paint to facilitate adding it in small amounts to her paints whenever necessary. Names for acrylics vary from manufacturer to manufacturer.

Latex Flat House Paint: Although house paint is a good printing medium, it is sold only in large quantities, making it costly to buy the many colors Jackie's designs require. And since wall printing uses but a small amount of paint, you will have quarts of leftovers. However, flat latex house paint is a good choice for painting a background stripe. One quart should cover 450 square feet.

Japan Paint: Japan paint is pigment suspended in a quick-drying resinous varnish that contains little or no oil. This is the paint traditionally used for stencilling because it dries instantly and is amazingly durable, lasting 30 years or more. In contrast, acrylics and latex house paint survive 10 to 12 years. Japan paint is sold in small quantities especially for stencilling, but these colors are usually dull. Brighter colors are available, but since they are packaged for sign painters, they are sold by the quart. The best Japan paint is Super-Fine-Japan, made by T.J. Ronan Co., Inc. Super-Fine comes in small cans and is available in some bright colors. Look for Japan paint in house-paint supply shops, hobby shops, and art-supply outlets.

One problem with Japan paint is that it accumulates in the template. If you aren't able to finish printing, you must thoroughly clean the template, or the crusted paint will flake off the next time you print and produce a jagged edge in the design.

Small amounts of artists' oils can be mixed with Japan paint to achieve a variety of colors, but if too much oil is added, the Japan paint will lose its quick-drying properties.

Illus. 1. Types of paint that can be used for wall-printing, left to right: Japan paint, oil base; alkyd enamel, oil base; latex enamel, water base; latex flat, water base; artists' acrylic, water base; metallics, lacquer base.

Japan paint is thinned and cleaned with turpentine or mineral spirits (Illus. 2). Cleanup takes about 45 minutes, as opposed to five minutes for water-based paints.

Illus. 2. Solvents for cleaning oil-based paints and metallics are from left: Lacquer thinner; Turpatene (turpentine substitute) and mineral spirits; along with wire brush used to break dried paint out of brush bristles.
Protectants for finished wallprints in heavy soil or moisture areas are from center to right.

Oils: It is a bad idea to use artists' oils alone. They are sold in convenient-to-use tubes, come in many more colors than Japan paint, and compare in durability to Japan paint. However, they take a long time to dry. This can be most inconvenient, because it means you have to wait several minutes for each part of the print to dry before you can print anything that overlaps it. In addition, oils are transparent, which enables the wall color to show through.

You can speed drying time by mixing oils with white Japan paint or Japan drier, which are available at art dealers. White Japan will make oils more opaque as well.

No design in this book can be printed in oil alone without great difficulty, except the ferns. Also, as with the Japan paints, cleanup is time-consuming.

PAPER TOWELS
For cleanup and wiping brushes.

PLASTIC PLATES
Plastic plates make great palettes. If you use oil-based or Japan paints, don't use Styrofoam (expanded polystyrene) plates; they dissolve in turpentine or mineral spirits (Illus. 3).

PLASTIC SPOONS
Use one to mix each paint color.

12

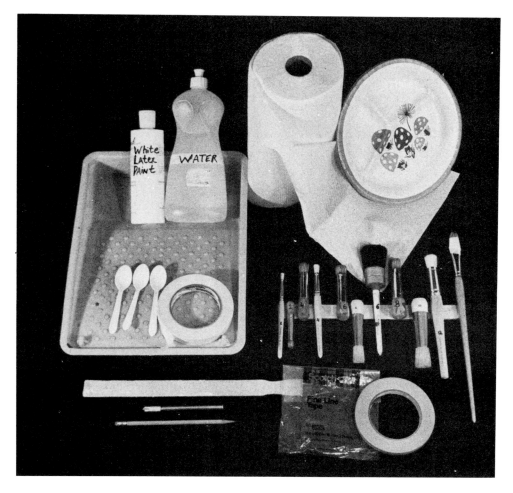

Illus. 3. General palette set up: Roller tray for holding palette, water and white paint; plastic spoons to mix paints; masking tape for template hinges, make unsticky before using. Squeeze bottles—for water-based paint. Paper towels for general clean-up and dry brush and transparent veining techniques; plastic or wax coated paper plates for palettes; stencil and artist brushes 3M Fine Line tape for taping off background stripe. X-Acto knife— general use; pencil for marking; stir stick.

STENCIL BRUSHES

Special brushes designed specifically for stencilling are sold in art-supply shops. They have stiff bundles of bristles (all of equal length) so that the stenciller can apply paint with short brisk strokes. They look like old-fashioned shaving brushes and range in size from that of a small human finger to a broom handle or even larger. Small brushes are good for fine details, while large ones speed the printing of big, open areas. Jackie prefers natural bristles—horsehair, pig hair, etc.—because she finds that they hold paint better, are more responsive, and excel in printing fine detail. The brushes you choose should feel soft and flexible.

You can make your own stencil brushes from square, flat artist's brushes called *flats* by binding the bristles with masking tape from their stem to halfway down their length (Illus. 4).

You will need one brush for each color in the wall print—especially if you use an oil-based paint. This is because the brushes must not only be washed but also dried if you plan to use them to apply another color. Any wetness from water or solvent on the brush dilutes the paint and sometimes causes it to bleed. A brush used on oil-based paint can be dried properly only by time—overnight at least. Brushes cleaned with water can be dried at once with some patience and effort by alternately slinging the brush and then vigorously wiping it on paper towels.

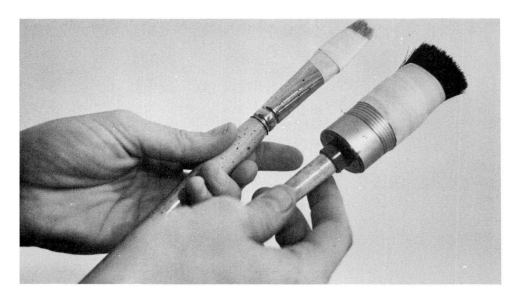

Illus. 4. An artist's square flat brush can be wrapped with masking tape and used as a stencil brush (left). Traditional stencil brush shape is round with bristles all one length (right).

Suggestions are given with each design for the number and sizes of brushes you will need. The suggestions are based upon printing the design without washing any brushes but using the same brush for similar colors.

WIRE BRUSH
This looks like a hairbrush except the bristles are made of wire. It is used to clean the stencil brushes and is sold at hardware dealers.

STENCIL BOARD OR CLEAR (POLYESTER) MYLAR
Stencil board is thick, oiled or waxed paper; clear Mylar is thin sheet plastic (Illus. 5) Both are used to make stencil templates—the stiff sheets of material into which the design is cut.

Polyester (not acetate) frosted Mylar is the best choice for the borders in this book. The main reason is that it is translucent, which makes transferring the design and registration (alignment of the template)

Illus. 5. Template materials (counter-clockwise from lower left): Stencil board in various thicknesses; polyester Mylar X-Acto knife; transparent tape for fixing miscuts; masking tape to hold pattern to material; typing carbons for transferring pattern template, if stencil board. Cutting pad to protect cutting surface and keep blade of knife from dulling; pencil for tracing to get a composite; ball-point pen for transferring pattern.

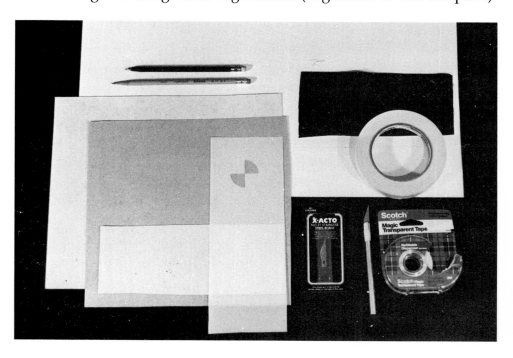

simpler. As you print, you can see through the Mylar to help line up the layers of images that make the design. And Mylar is easier to cut. In addition, Mylar lasts indefinitely, whereas stencil board breaks down around delicate shapes after about 25 prints. In fact, if you make more than 25 images of the design on the wall and choose to use stencil board, you probably will have to cut a duplicate template for all the delicate areas.

Also, Mylar is slightly less expensive. It is sold from rolls by the yard at architecture- or art-supply shops. (Mylar is occasionally available in sheets as well.) It should be 0.005 or 0.004 gauge and frosted on one or both sides. A further problem with stencil board is that it is sometimes available only in small sheets. Check to make sure the size you purchase is big enough for your design.

Mylar's only disadvantage is that it is sometimes curly and needs extra taping to the wall to lie flat for printing.

If you use stencil board, buy the thinnest available; it lasts as long as thicker material and is easier to cut. Stencil board is sold at art-supply and hobby shops.

KNIFE

Cut Mylar or stencil board with a sharp X-acto knife (available at art-supply or hobby shops) or similar tool. Use a No. 1 handle with a No. 11 blade. Purchase extra blades, as it takes about three to cut a stencil. Jackie prefers the No. 11 blade because its tiny point is good for delicate cutting. Some people, however, find they keep breaking the little tip and so prefer to use the No. 1 handle with the No. 24 blade. Other manufacturers make similar knives that may be numbered differently but which should work equally as well. Don't get a swivel blade knife, which is sold for frisket cutting (a silk-screen process). It is not strong enough to cut Mylar, and the average person cannot control its swivelling.

TABLE PROTECTION

To protect the table from the blade of the knife as you cut the template, use matboard (heavy pasteboard) purchased from an art-supply shop or two thicknesses of cardboard from the back of a notebook taped together, or some similar material. Art or framing shops will sometimes give you scraps of matboard that they normally would throw away. A 12 × 16-inch piece is a good size. Don't use a piece of glass or plastic for protection. Glass will break the knife point; plastic will dull it.

CARBON PAPER

If you make templates with stencil board, use carbon paper to transfer the design from the book to the stencil board. You will need to assemble several sheets of ordinary typewriter carbon paper to make a piece big enough to accommodate the design. Tape the sheets together with transparent tape on the noncarbon side of the sheets. If you use Mylar, you don't need carbon paper.

FROSTED TRANSPARENT TAPE

Jackie uses Scotch Magic frosted transparent tape to fix stencil-cutting mistakes on both Mylar and stencil board. It comes in handy for other reasons as well.

MASKING TAPE

One-inch masking tape is used to bind brushes and hold stencils to the wall.

AUTOMOTIVE TAPE

Used to stripe cars, this tape is available at mechanics' shops as well as at automotive and commercial paint-supply dealers. It is used to mask out the wall if you wish to paint a background stripe, a small line under your design, an overlining stripe, or two narrow stripes on either edge of the border to enclose it. Fine-line tape comes in various widths: buy the ½-inch size.

CHALK LINE

A chalk line is used to mark out a background stripe, if you decide to use one.

PENCIL, RULER, AND STRAIGHTEDGE

These are for marking the path of the border. A chalk line is used to mark a background stripe only.

MINERAL SPIRITS OR TURPENTINE

Thin and clean oil-based paints, such as artists' oils or Japan paint, with either of these solvents. Water-based paints are, of course, cleaned with water.

Wall Preparation

As with any kind of printing, the surface that receives the image must be carefully chosen.

The smoothest walls produce the [cleanest] [clearest] prints. On rougher surfaces, the edges of the images will blur, or worse yet, the paint may bleed underneath the template.

It is best to wall-print upon a freshly painted wall. Then the new border won't make the rest of the wall look dirty. And you can save some of the paint to touch up mistakes. If you decide not to paint, at least scrub down the room with a good cleaning solution (Illus. 6).

The paint on the wall should be durable and compatible with the paint you will use to wall-print. The rules for matching wall paint and print paint are:

1. The oil-base family of wall paints—flat, semigloss, and gloss—can only be printed with the oil-base family of print paints—artists' oils and Japan paint.
2. The latex family of wall paints—flat, semigloss, and glossy—can be printed with all of the paints listed in the materials list.
3. All glossy and semigloss surfaces, whether oil or latex, must be

dulled before printing. Do this by *lightly* sanding the area to be printed with sandpaper (Nos. 220 or 300) or steel wool (size 00) until the gloss is dulled, leaving a matt finish.

Of all the types of wall paint, flat latex provides the best base, because it is extremely porous and therefore absorbs the wall print better.

A flat latex is a bad choice, however, for a room that endures much grease, moisture, or scrubbing, such as a kitchen, bathroom, or nursery, unless you varnish the walls to seal out moisture. In these rooms, you may wish to paint walls with either a flat oil-based paint or a semigloss or gloss paint in either oil or latex.

If you are faced with a wall that has been scribbled on with ink markers or that has other stains that may seep through a new coat of paint, you can apply a primer-sealer to the stained area.

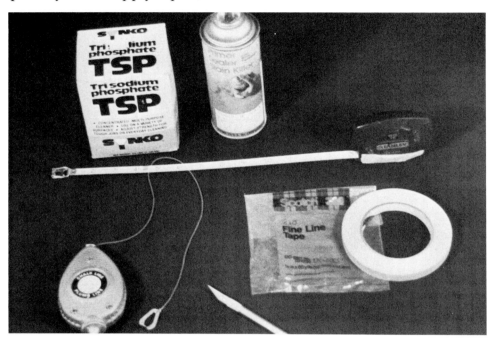

Illus. 6.   Materials for wall preparation (clockwise from upper left): T.S.P., strong commercial wall cleaner; primer sealer, to cover any strong stains on wall; measuring tape; tape for applying background or edge stripes. X-Acto knife for trimming tape; snap chalk line for drawing long lines for background stripes; yardstick for measuring.

To Lay a Background Stripe

Wall-printed borders usually look best with a background stripe underneath. It helps define the border and produces a finished look. To lay a stripe, you need a chalk line or a pencil, ruler, and straightedge. Consult the special instructions for your design for the width of the border. Decide how much wider than the design you want the background stripe to be. For example, you could make the background stripe ½ inch wider than the width of the border. This would allow ¼ inch extra on both sides of the border.

Before you lay the stripe, read Sizing the Print to Fit the Room (page 18) to determine the path of the border. Then, measuring down from the ceiling or up from the floor (whichever is closest to the border), mark and draw a line with a chalk line or straightedge to define both edges of the border. If you use a chalk line, remove most of the chalk before you snap the line by rubbing the line over a paper towel.

Carefully cover the two lines with 3M Fine-Line automotive tape, #6303, ½ inch wide. Don't press the tape too firmly, or it will pull off the wall paint when removed. Then paint in the stripe. The paint used for the stripe must be compatible with both the paint on the wall and the paint you will use to print the design. See rules 1 and 2 under Wall Preparation (page 16).

Miniborders

Three miniborders—simple, narrow stencilled bands—are included in this book and have been designed to combine with the larger borders. The special instructions for each larger design include suggestions for choosing a companion miniborder.

The fern with the arched border is a good example of how a miniborder can complement a larger border.

Sizing the Print to Fit the Room

Almost all of the borders are designed so that the stenciller can engineer them to fit precisely within the space available. This makes it possible for the beginning of the border design to meet the end without leaving a seam.

To expand or shrink the borders for a good fit, employ either of the following two methods. The chief technique applied to almost all the designs is called a *flexible repeat*. It is similar to the seam allowance on a dress pattern. The pattern is "let out" at the seams. With each design, specific figures are given for its flexible repeat.

In addition to this first method, six of the patterns—nasturtium, forget-me-not, begonia, calla lily, daffodil, and California poppy—require the stenciller to fill gaps in the border with a random element, which is a small design compatible with the larger border, that can be inserted wherever you wish (Illus. 7). The borders with random elements cannot be expanded nearly as much as the others. This is why the random element was included.

The fern is an exception to all of the above because it does not repeat. The fronds are simply applied at random, making this design the easiest to print.

Sizing a design to a room takes some imagination and some mathematical computation. First, turn to the specific instructions for the design you have chosen and read the height of the border, the range within which it can be made to repeat flexibly, and whether it contains a random element.

Then examine the room where the border will be printed. For a border planned for the top of a wall, measure the space between the ceiling and any interruptions, such as windows and doors, to see if the design fits (Illus. 8). If the border is too wide, you may want to print it lower on the wall so that the top of the design is lower than the top of the lowest window or door. Then, when you wall-print, you will stop the design when it reaches the window and then continue it on the other side. Or, you may decide instead to print the design so that the top is a bit higher than the windows, curling the border over the corners of them, perhaps using the random element to complete the curl. For wainscot or floor borders, you have less choice. You must break off printing when you hit openings in the wall and then continue on the other side of them.

After you decide how to position the print on the wall, measure its entire path in inches.

Now, in order for your design to meet itself seamlessly, you have to size the stencil template so that its length in inches—the number of inches it runs before it repeats—matches evenly the path of the border in inches.

Illus. 7. Insertion and printing of forget-me-not random element. Random elements are provided with some of the patterns to help in fitting pattern specifications to your room size.

Illus. 8. Windows and doors are considerations when planning path of border design. The amount of design showing on the left side of the window is more pleasant to the eye than the little blurbs of design isolated above the window on the right.

Here is an example of how you might make this decision. If the circumference of the room you plan to print is 312 inches and the pattern has a flexible repeat of every 14 to 17 inches, you must discover if 14, 15, 16, or 17 will divide evenly into 312. Divide 312 by 14. It goes 22 times, with 4 inches left over. Try 15. It goes 20 times with 12 inches left over. Neither 16 nor 17 goes evenly, either. So you decide to go for 15, rather arbitrarily.

You already know that a 15-inch repeat will print the image 20 times in the room with 12 inches left over. So the perfect template would be somewhat larger than 15 inches. To decide exactly how large to make the repeat, divide the circumference to be printed by the number of repeats you have already roughly determined—divide 312 by 20 in this case. Carry out the division to one decimal. In this case, you discover that the stencil should be expanded to 15.6 inches for a precise fit (15.6 equals 15⁶⁄₁₀, which equals 15⅗ inches).

Or, if fractions boggle your mind, you could print at the 15-inch repeat 14 times, and at 17 inches 6 times. Scatter the larger repeats evenly around the room to make them less noticeable.

The expansion is accomlpished by moving the registration marks on the templates when you cut them. Further instructions are given in the section on Cutting.

In the case of the patterns that employ random elements, divide the circumference as above but use the random elements to fill in leftover inches. The sizes of the random elements are given in the special instructions for these patterns.

Making Templates

The borders shown in this book are big—bigger than the 8½- by 11-inch format of the book. Therefore, to make most of the templates, you must assemble several pages of the book. To aid you in piecing the puzzle together, pages are labelled "Print 1, Part A" or "Print 1, Part B," etc. A miniature drawing of each complete template is given with the design.

To make the templates, first trace onto tracing paper (Illus. 9) or copy on a copy machine all the pages involved in your design. If you use a copy machine or have the pages copied at a commercial print shop, be sure the pages lie flat on the machine (but avoid breaking the book's spine). Use a good-quality copy machine that will not distort the design.

Assemble the pages into templates on a sunny window in the following fashion:

Tape "Print 1, Part A" to the window with frosted transparent tape. Use only two small pieces of tape, one at each top corner of the page. Next, tape "Print 1, Part B" onto the window, aligning it with "Print 1, Part A" as described below. Again, only tape the page to the window by its top two corners. *Do not tape the pages to each other.*

Bring the half circles with **V**'s on each page together to form complete circles with **X**'s in them. The dotted lines between the circles should fall directly on top of each other (Illus. 10). On some of the pages, parts of the design are outlined with dots, instead of colored in as solid black shapes like most of the design. These dots mark overlapping parts of the design. When the pages are lined up properly, the areas outlined in dots will fall directly over the same shape in solid black on the other page.

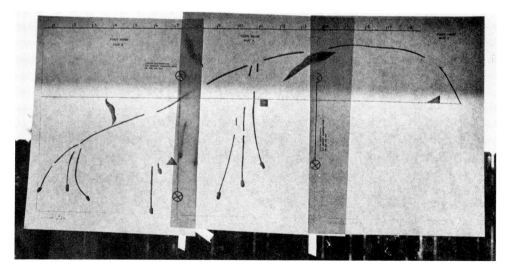

Illus. 10. Parts A, B, and C of first print are assembled on windows and taped at top edge. Pieces are fitted together by aligning circles and lines on top of each other.

If it is labelled "Print 1, Part C," place it alongside its companion pages and tape it also to the window.

Then, compose the second template. The trick is to do this directly on top of the first template already on the window, allowing you to make sure the registration marks between the templates line up. The registration marks are geometric shapes inside the design and at the bottom of the pages. They are triangles, squares, double squares, rectangles. When the registration marks are properly aligned, all the images on the templates will fall together correctly (Illus. 11). Again, tape the pages to the window only, not to each other, and use only small hinges of tape at the top of the pages. This will enable you to make adjustments easily as you add pages.

Illus. 11. Matching registration marks—square and triangle—of second print with registration of first print. The real test of alignment is that the leaves fall on the stem.

Continue to layer the templates on the window, lining up all registration marks (Illus. 12–13). It is important to layer the templates on the window in the order they will be printed—print 1, print 2, print 3, etc.—as indicated on the pages.

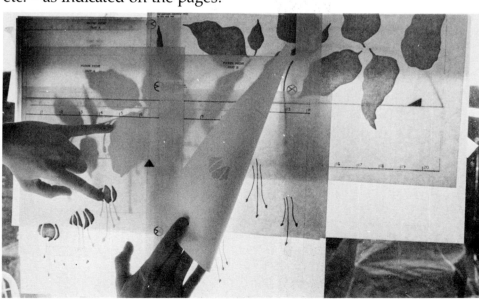

Illus. 12. Montage of photocopies successfully aligned, creates the design in layer upon layer. This is the fourth layer.

When all the pages are positioned on the window, it is time to tape the pages together to form the templates. Be careful not to tape the wrong pages together. Tape "Print 1, Part A" to "Print 1, Part B" to "Print 1, Part C," and so forth to make the first template; the "Print 2, Part A" to "Print 2, Part B" to "Print 2, Part C" to make the second template, and so forth. Make sure that the whole pile stays aligned as you work. Tape the pages along the entire length where they join.

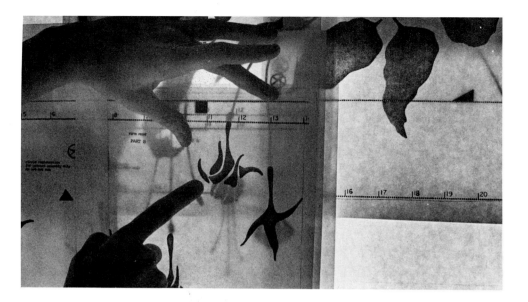

Illus. 13. Fifth print of fuchsia aligns top of flower with bottom petals. Note baseline (line connecting square with triangle) matches on all five layers of prints.

Transferring the Design

If you are making your templates with stencil board, use carbon paper to transfer each template pattern to its own sheet of stencil board. Make a piece of carbon paper as big as the design by taping several sheets together with transparent tape on the "clean," or non-carbon, side of the carbon paper. Cut a piece of stencil board big enough to accommodate the design and leave at least a 1-inch frame of board around the entire edge. Tape the pattern to the stencil board along the top edge. Slip the carbon paper between the design and the stencil board, carbon side down (Illus. 14). Trace around all the solid black shapes with a ballpoint pen. Be sure to trace the registration marks as well as the design (Illus. 15).

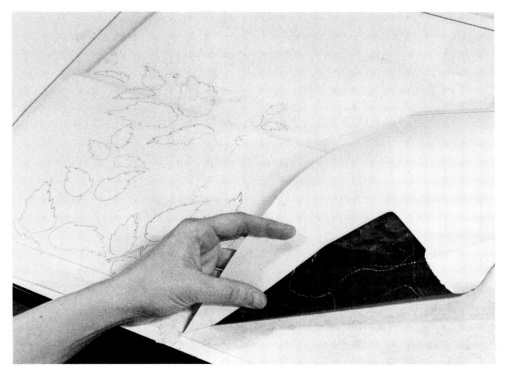

Illus. 14. Layers of traced or photocopied pattern, carbon paper and stencil board ready to be transferred. Circles and line registrations are not traced; they act as guides to assemble pieces of pattern into template layers. Registration marks are to be printed.

23

Illus. 15. Design transferred to stencil board by carbon. It is now ready to cut out. Note that registration marks are transferred and circles and lines are not transferred.

If you make templates from frosted Mylar, skip the tracing step with the carbon. Instead, cut a piece of Mylar big enough to allow a 1-inch frame around the template design. Next, place the Mylar on top of the copied design so that you can see the design through the Mylar. Make sure the frosted side of the Mylar faces upwards. Tape the design securely underneath the Mylar, along all its edges (Illus. 16). Then cut the design, as described in Cutting (the next section). Repeat these steps for all templates.

Illus. 16. When using Mylar as template material, traced or photocopied patterns can be taped directly to shiny side of Mylar and then cut out.

Cutting

Whether you use stencil board or Mylar, the cutting instructions are the same. Cut the template with the X-acto knife, or a facsimile of an X-acto knife, using the matboard or cardboard pad to protect the worktable (Illus. 17). It is easier to cut by pulling the knife towards you. Take

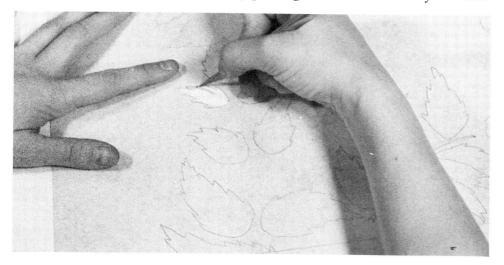

Illus. 17. Cutting template on top of cutting pad. It is easier to cut and you have better control of knife tip if as you cut, you pull knife towards you.

care not to cut yourself. If you turn the template as your work, you will be able to make most of your cuts in this easier manner. The minute the knife ceases to cut with ease, change the blade. To negotiate tight corners, first perforate them with the tip of the knife, then cut.

It is important to cut precisely the registration marks—the triangles, squares, and rectangles at the bottom of each stencil plate. If you cut the first registration mark on the inside of the lines, cut all of them that way. If you cut on the outside the first time, cut all of them that way (Illus. 18).

Illus. 18. For an expansion that will take place with every printing, permanently move the right registration mark over the precalculated amount and cut out.

At this point you should move the registration marks if you want to expand the repeating section of the pattern. You do this by moving one of the side-by-side registration marks, which are the matching pair of geometrical shapes at the bottom of the template, one at each side. They are drawn in the book for the smallest repeat. For a larger repeat, move one member of the pair over as much as you want to expand. Be careful not to make the repeat larger than suggested.

Just change the repeat on the first template. The other templates will line up with the first.

If your knife skitters off track, making an errant slice, you can fix it with frosted transparent tape. Stick tape to both the front and back of the mistake and then recut to remove excess tape (Illus. 19). The same remedy applies if you remove more of the stencil board or Mylar than you should. Use a layer of tape front and back to fill in the gap, press the two layers firmly together, then recut. See Illus. 20–22 for more cutting tips.

Because Mylar is translucent, it is difficult to see cutting mistakes. When you are finished cutting, hold the template against something

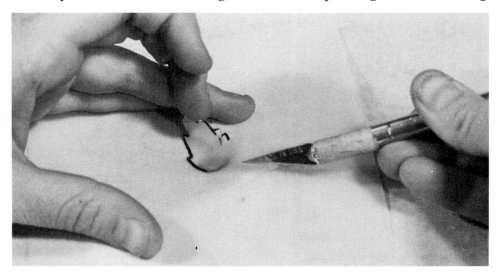

Illus. 19. Mistakes in cutting template can be easily repaired by applying Scotch Magic tape to both sides of template, then recutting correctly.

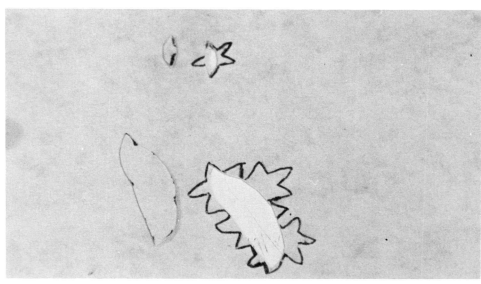

Illus. 20. When you have a jagged shape to cut, it helps to cut largest area of shape first. The tiny flowers of the forget-me-not can be cut out quickly by cutting an oval shape out first then cutting the other petals as described in text.

26

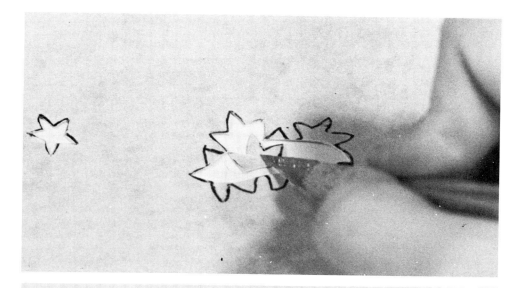

Illus. 21. After cutting center area out, you can easily trim edges of shape by rotating template and cutting towards the open center.

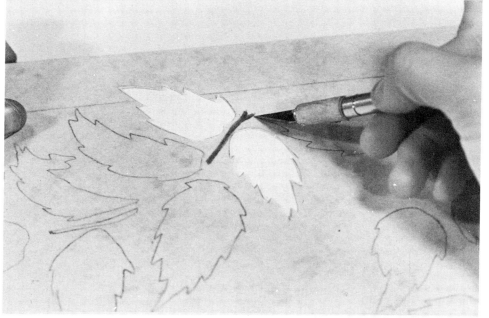

Illus. 22. Cut delicate shapes last. Use a sharp, new blade and take your time. If you tire of cutting delicate shapes, take a break and cut some of the larger areas of another template.

black. This will enable you to see rough edges and spots where you have overcut. Fix these as described above.

The templates must be printed in the order given in the book (Print 1, first, then Print 2, etc.). To keep track of the order, write in pencil the correct print number on the front of the template after you cut it. Also, pencil the word *top* in the appropriate place.

Making a Tracing

Give a final check to the design before printing it by tracing it in its entirety on a large sheet of paper with colored pencils. Trace the templates in the order they will be printed, including registration marks.

If the templates line up beautifully, but the registration marks don't, recut registration marks so that when positioned exactly on top of each other, they will cause the design to assemble correctly.

If the design doesn't fall together as it should, find out which template is causing the problem. Put template 2 on template 1. Then trace 2 directly onto 1. They should line up. Next, trace template 3 onto 1 and check it for alignment. Continue until you identify the faulty templates. You can usually fix the problem with just a little recutting (Illus. 23).

Don't use soft-tipped pens for the tracing step because they will stain the inside edges of the template; the color may later bleed into the work as you print.

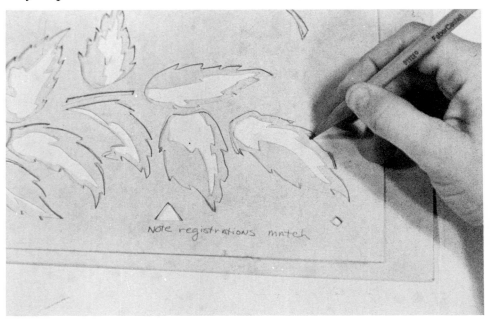

Illus. 23. Tracing all templates with pencil onto first template helps to locate which one may need a little trimming. Remember, if you have cut too much out, you can apply transparent tape and recut.

Printing

Gather brushes, palettes (plastic plates), paint, water or other solvent, paper towels, templates, and masking tape.

To apply a ceiling border, you need a ladder or some sort of scaffolding. Jackie's feet ache when she stands on the rung of a ladder all day, so she makes a temporary scaffolding from a wide plank supported by two sturdy chairs. Take care that whatever you stand on is sturdy and safe.

Before you start printing, you need a baseline on the wall to help you print the first template. After the first template is printed, it will guide the position of all the rest.

If you use a background stripe, then it can serve as a baseline. Mark the two edges of the stripe on the first template in the proper positions. You will have two parallel pencilled lines going across the entire template, marking the track of the background stripe. As you print, match the pencilled lines to the background stripe.

If there is no background stripe, make a baseline as follows. All of the designs except the fuchsia have a distinct bottom edge where the stems all end. (To line up the fuchsia, follow special instructions given with that design.) Draw the baseline in pencil using a straightedge and ruler, where you wish the bottom of the pattern to run. Mark the position of the line, measuring down from the ceiling or up from the floor, whichever is closer. Then join the marks in pencil, using a straight-edge. Make the pencilled line light, for easier removal later. Do not use a chalk line to mark the baseline, because sometimes the chalk will bleed into your design.

In most cases, the first template printed has cutouts that fall along the bottom edge of the design. As you print, you will be able to see through the cutouts to align the bottom of the design along the base-line. However, in the cases of the nasturtium, calla lily, and forget-me-not, the first template does not print to the bottom edge of the design. For these designs, you must take the second template, fit it over the first, and mark the bottom edge of the design onto the first with pencil. Join those marks with a straightedge, extending the line entirely across the template (Illus. 24). As you stencil the first template, match the pencilled line on the template to the baseline. With stencil board, match the baseline to where the pencilled line hits the edges of the template. With the Mylar, you will be able to see through the template to match up the baseline along its entire length.

To prepare your brushes for printing, firmly wrap masking tape down half the length of their bristles, starting where the bristles join the brush handle. This will cause the brushes to stencil better and make them easier to clean.

You are now ready to print. Start at a wall section where you seldom look when entering or sitting in the room. Also, start in the middle of a wall, not in a corner.

The template is held in place with masking tape while you print. Masking tape can pull the paint off the wall if it is too sticky. So make your own unsticky masking tape by taking a short (3- to 5-inch) strip of tape, sticking it to your clothing, and then pulling it off.

Illus. 24. Mark where the baseline falls on the template with pencil and apply transparent tape over it to protect line from being rubbed or washed off. To print repeat of pattern template, match registration cutouts from previous print and align baseline markings so they overlap.

Attach a strip of tape to all four corners of the template. To make it easier to remove the template after each print, make a pull tab by turning over a little "hem" at the end of each piece of tape (Illus. 25). Align the template on the baseline, stick down the top tape hinges, but don't tape down the bottom ones yet.

Illus. 25. Masking tape hinges with tabs made by folding end of tape onto itself are attached to top and bottom of template. Other small tape pieces can go on sides to keep Mylar templates from curling away from wall.

Before you tape down the bottom hinges, you need to place tiny pieces of masking tape directly underneath where the registration marks will print. This will keep the registration marks from actually printing on the wall. If you printed them on the wall, you would have to paint them out later with paint the same color as the wall. So figure out where the registration marks are going to print, and then put little pieces of masking tape there. Be careful not to accidentally put the tape on areas that will be printed with the design. Make the tapes barely big enough to accommodate the registration marks (Illus. 26).

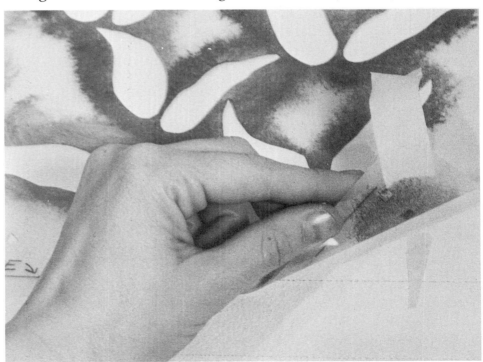

Illus. 26. Apply small pieces of unsticky masking tape where registration marks will fall. Keep pieces small so they will not be in the way of printing the pattern.

30

After the registration marks are provided for, apply the bottom tapes. For large patterns you may have to secure the template with additional pieces of tape. It is important that the template be firmly held to the wall.

Following the special instructions for your design, load the brush with a small amount of paint. To print, the brush should be fairly dry, holding little paint. Unload excess paint on a spare corner of the template. You can use this excess paint later to refill your brush. Further reduce the amount of paint on the brush by wiping it on a paper towel.

With short, firm strokes, brush paint into all the cutout areas of the design, including the registration marks. Don't worry about carefully staying within the lines of the cutouts. You will get a better print with crisper edges if you allow the brush to stroke onto the template. Gently lift the template after you have printed a bit to see how the work is going. Some templates are printed with more than one color; others are printed twice. Consult the special instructions for your design.

When you finish, carefully remove the template. Now position the template for a second print. Again, line it up with the baseline on the wall. Also, space it the proper distance away from the first print. Remember that registration marks include a pair of matching geometric shapes, one on each side of the template. These are the side-to-side registration marks, used to link the prints on the wall. Place the template approximately where you wish to print it, then align it more precisely by placing the nearest side-to-side registration mark so that it falls on top of a side-to-side registration mark you have just printed. As you continue to print the template, continue to link the side-to-side registration marks (Illus. 27).

Illus. 27. Position template so that left registration holes fall on top of the print of the right registrations.

If you plan to make use of random elements, leave a spot for them as you work. Slide the template farther along the baseline—instead of lining up the side-to-side registration marks—to make room for the element. It is easiest to print the random element when you are using its color of paint on the larger part of the design.

If you use quick-drying paint, you may want to print one section of the room entirely with all the templates before moving on. This makes the work more interesting and saves frequent moving of the ladder and scaffolding.

To print the second part of the design, match the registration marks on the second template with those already on the wall. If you are wall-printing with Mylar, you will be able to see through the template to further adjust the print. Secure the stencil with its tapes. Using a brush that is perfectly clean and dry, print as with the first template. (See Cleanup step on page 35 for brush-cleaning and -drying techniques.) If you are printing the second template with the same family of color as the first, you can reuse the brush without washing it. Simply wipe off as much of the paint as possible.

In the same manner, print all of the templates for your design in the correct order.

As she prints, Jackie usually stores the templates not in use by taping them to the wall below her work.

Obstacles

When you are printing a corner, it is difficult to get the template firmly enough against the wall. For inside corners, press the template firmly into the depression. For outside corners, wrap it around the protrusion. Then bind it to the wall with extra pieces of tape. Tape one side of the corner and then the other, as you line up the baseline and side-to-side registration. To keep the stencil from wiggling, hold it down with your hand as you paint.

If the path of the border hits windows and doors, print as much of the template as you can, right up to the edge of the opening. Then print the rest of the template on the other side of the opening.

Almost Finished

When you are six or seven prints short of completing the room's perimeter, check to see if you are going to come out evenly as planned. Do this by taking template No. 1 and measuring out the remaining distance, using a pencil to correctly link the side-by-side registration as you go. If measurements are off, you can make allowances by shortening or lengthening the side-to-side registration or inserting an additional random element. When you are finished, remove the registration marks and touch up with background paint and a small artist's brush (Illus. 28) any places where the design bled under the template. Also use background paint to cover the pencilled baseline. (Merely erasing the line will leave a track with a different sheen.)

Special Effects

Jackie makes her designs look more like paintings and less like stencils by employing the following techniques. Rather than simply putting a flat coat of paint in the stencil, she varies the effect by mottling, speckling, or shading. Here are some of her tricks:

Two-tone Mottling: Load the brush with two different colors of paint, one in each corner. As the printing proceeds, favor first one and then the other color, producing a cloudy effect.

Dry-brush Shading (Illus. 29): Load the brush with paint, but then pounce and feather it on paper towels until almost all of the paint is removed and the brush marks a pattern of dots.

Illus. 28. Any bleeds of paint around the image can be painted out with extra background paint using a small #2 artists' round brush.

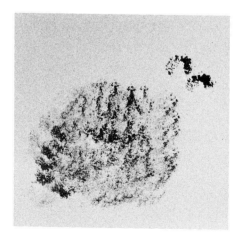

Illus. 29. Dry brush shading: Use a pouncing motion to tap the bristles on the wall surface. The brush should print in speckles fairly evenly.

33

Then pounce the dry brush into the cutouts to produce a soft overcast of speckles or flecks, as in the forget-me-not design. Or, as in the calla lily, even more paint can be removed from the brush, to give a finer haze of speckles, which are used for shading. Or, as in the case of the rose, the dry brush is swirled upon the wall, along the edges of the cutouts, for a soft shading effect.

Illus. 30.   Dry brush shading: The rose pattern utilizes a dry brush to softly pull pink from edges into center which has already been printed with yellow. Instead of a pouncing motion, this requires a swirling motion to achieve the soft blending.

Transparent Veining (Illus. 31): To create lifelike veins in the fuchsia design, apply thin green paint—almost "green water"—to leaves after they have been stencilled a basic green. Brush on the paint with an artists' rounded flat brush, following the contours real veins might take. The central vein is painted first, then the side veins are pulled in from the edge of the leaf towards the center vein.

Illus. 31.   Transparent veining: After printing the leaf green, make veins by painting thin green lines with thinned green paint.

Metallics: You may want to add sparkle to your border with metallic paints. These are sold as bronze powders suspended in a lacquer-type base. Just use the sediment at the bottom of the jar, not the suspension liquid. Mix about ½ teaspoon (2 mL) of the sediment with 3 (45 mL) tablespoons of varnish or shellac. The varnish or shellac is used to seal the powders from the outside air. Otherwise, the metallics will tarnish, producing an unattractive look. Don't use a plastic spoon to dip out the sediment as the liquid will melt it, and only mix a small amount at a time. Use the metallics as you would any other paint, but apply them with discretion. Too much can look fake and vulgar. But used subtly, as in a tiny gilt edge to a larger stripe, the metallics produce a royal, formal feeling.

Cleanup

Remove the masking tape binding the bristles of each stencil brush by slicing through it with your knife and then peeling it off. Using the wire brush, brush the paint out of the stencil brush (Illus. 32). Then completely clean each brush with the proper solvent.

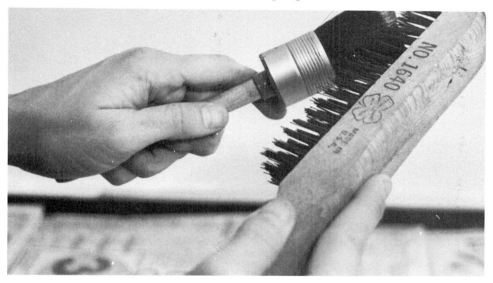

Illus. 32. Use the wire brush to loosen paint from bristles of brush.

Clean oil-based paints with mineral spirits or turpentine. Use the two-can method. Take two coffee cans that have lids. Put two inches of solvent into each can. After you have loosened the paint with the wire brush, dip the brush into the first can and then wipe it off on newspapers. Continue to dip, wipe, dip, wipe, until the brush is almost clean. Then switch to the second coffee can and repeat the process. You need the second can of clean turpentine because you can only get a brush as clean as your turpentine or mineral spirits are.

When you are finished, pour the solvent from the second coffee can into the first can and snap on lids of both cans. When you need to clean a brush again, put clean solvent into the second can and repeat the procedure from the beginning. A brush must be perfectly dry before it can be used again. Otherwise, any solvent that remains on the bristles may dilute the paint and cause the print to bleed. With mineral spirits and turpentine, the brush must be left to dry overnight before it is used again.

If you have used latex house paint, acrylics, or other water-based paint, clean the brushes with soap and water. Brushes cleaned with soap and water can be adequately dried for use again the same day. Do this by alternately slinging the water from the brush and energetically wiping it on paper towels until the bristles are bone-dry. Remember to retape the bristles with masking tape before painting again with the brush.

If you use Japan paint, you will need to clean the stencils as well as the brushes if you wish to reuse them. Wipe them down with paper towels or newspapers that have been dipped in solvent. Loosen the paint and remove it. If you have used stencil board, be careful not to let the board get soaked with solvent as you work.

Other kinds of paint will build up on the template, but you can ignore this as they will not flake off if the templates are used later. However, you may wish to remove paint with an X-acto knife from delicate parts of the stencil as they become clogged. Turn the template back side up. You will be able to see to cut the excess paint from the template.

Protecting the Stencil

Wait at least two days before applying a protective finish to the stencilled border.

If the stencil is in a room and a position that receives little wear or moisture, there is no need to protect it. But if you wish, you can provide easy and adequate protection by spraying the border with a fixative, like the one artists use to fix charcoal drawings. The fixative comes in spray cans and is available at art-supply shops. Just spray it over the border. It will blend with either shiny or matt-finish wall paint.

For areas that receive wear or moisture, clear varnish is a good protector. Use the clearest you can find. Match the sheen of the varnish to that of the wall. That is, if the wall is painted with flat latex paint, use a flat no-sheen varnish. If it is a glossy wall, apply a high-gloss varnish.

Apply only one light coat to the border area only. Mix four parts of varnish to one part of thinner. Load the brush, then wipe most of the varnish off; paint with an almost dry brush. Too much varnish on the brush will leave brush strokes or drips running down the wall. Don't worry about making straight edges where the varnish leaves off. Just feather the edges into the wall. The strokes will blend into the wall when the varnish dries.

Storing Stencil Brushes

Commercial painters store their brushes in brush sheaths to protect the bristles from curling. You can make a brush sheath for stencil brushes with masking tape and newspaper. Make a newspaper tube as wide as the widest part of your brush and a bit shorter than the brush in length. Seam and coat the tube with masking tape—one layer is enough. Store the brush in the sheath so that bristles are completely covered, but the handle is poking out. Hold the sheath in place with more masking tape (Illus. 33).

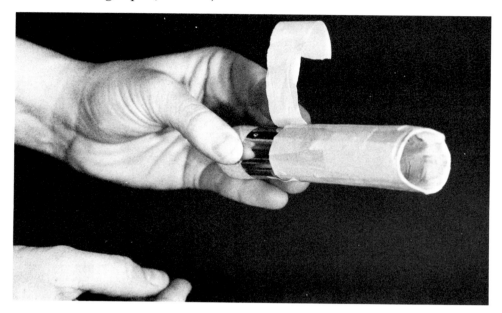

Illus. 33. Attach sheath to brush with a piece of tabbed masking tape.

Troubleshooting

Problem: Image bleeds on wall.

Solution: 1. Undetected extra cuts in the template let paint seep through where it shouldn't. Patch miscuts with transparent tape; apply to both sides of mistake.

2. You have put too much paint on the brush, or you are brushing it into the template too firmly. Try using less paint and pressure on the brush.

3. The template moved while you were printing. Try taping it down more securely.

4. The paint is too thin and runs under the template. Thicken paint to consistency of thin sour cream.

5. The wall surface is highly textured so that the paint puddles on the wall. Remember, the more highly textured the surface, the more difficult it is to print. Try using a dryer, less paint-laden brush.

6. Brush may have been moist from washing. The water or solvent on the brush mixed with the paint and caused it to bleed. Use a dry brush.

To repair bleeding mistakes on the wall, wipe off excess with paper towel if paint is still wet. After paint is dry, bleeds can be retouched with a small artist's brush and background paint.

Problem: Knife point keeps breaking when cutting template.

Solution: 1. If cutting pad has ridges, perhaps tip is getting caught in them. Use new cutting pad.

2. If you are using a glass-cutting pad, this may break the tip. Use cardboard or matboard pad.

3. Perhaps you are bearing down too hard on the knife tip only. Try holding the blade more horizontally instead of straight up.

4. Maybe you need a stronger blade. Try a No. 24 instead of a No. 11 X-acto blade.

Problem: The pattern is not registering correctly (for example, flowers and leaves are not being printed on top of stems).

Solution: Check all the templates to identify which one is not matching up with the rest. Line up images correctly and recut registration marks. For additional suggestions, see the section on Making a Tracing (page 27).

Problem: Room was sized inaccurately, and as a result the pattern does not meet evenly as planned.

Solution: Be sure to check for this possibility seven to ten prints before ending the border. You can fill in gaps with random elements or perhaps by changing the flexible repeat to fit the space that remains. You can make an emergency random element by printing just part of the pattern—maybe one flower or a part of a branch.

Patterns

BLACKBERRIES

The blackberry border is charming as wainscoting on a background stripe.

Tip for cutting "dots" for flower centers (print 3): First cut a triangle within the dot. Then round out the edges. The dots don't have to be perfectly round to look convincing. If you prefer, apply the dots with a No. 2 artist's round brush. Jackie finds this method equally as quick.

HEIGHT:

2⅜ inches

NUMBER OF TEMPLATES:

Three

TIME:

2 hours to transfer and cut; 7 minutes to print 3-foot section with complete image.

REPEAT:

6¾ inches. Cannot be sized to fit room except by leaving (small 11¼ inch) areas of open background randomly among printings. Have ends meet at obscure point on wall. Or, if border crosses openings in the wall, start and stop it at one to avoid showing a seam.

COLORS

Use acrylics unless noted otherwise.

Raw Umber	Naphthol Crimson
Yellow Ochre/Yellow Oxide	White latex
Hooker's Green	

BRUSHES:

Two No. 10 and two No. 4 stencil brushes.

PRINTING:

Print 1—Mix Raw Umber, Yellow Ochre and white to print stems with No. 10 stencil brush.

Print 2—Using white latex, print the flowers two times with the No. 10 stencil brush to ensure crisp blossoms. Use a No. 4 stencil brush to apply a diffused circle of Yellow Ochre to flower centers, using nearly dry brush. Prepare brush by loading it with Yellow Ochre and then pouncing on paper towels until the brush makes speckles.

Print 3—Print leaves using a No. 10 stencil brush with yellow-green created by mixing Yellow Ochre, Hooker's Green, and white. Print centers (dots) of flowers in red, using Naphthol Crimson on No. 4 stencil brush.

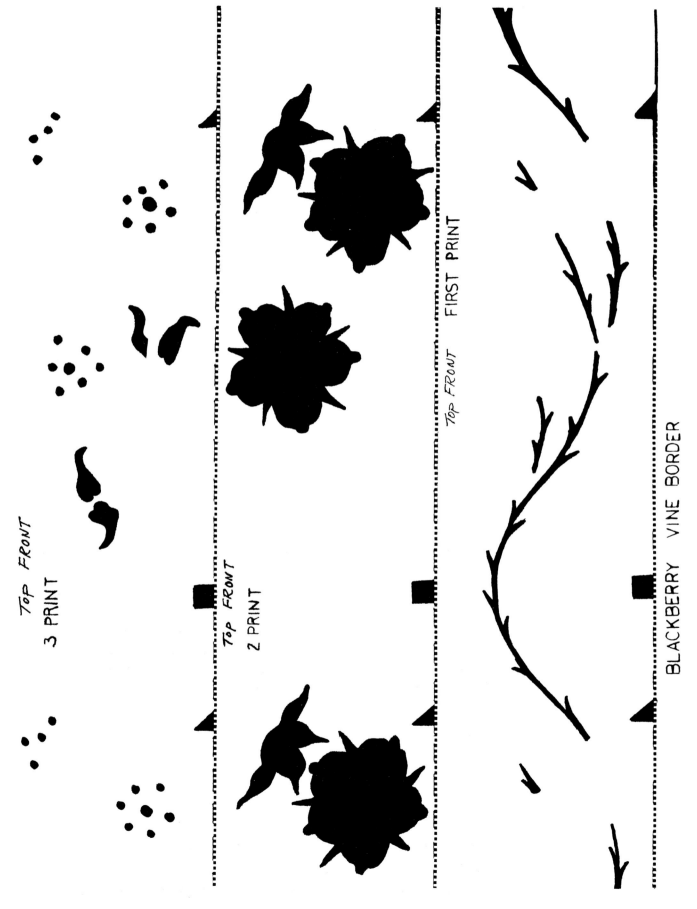

TOP FRONT
3 PRINT

TOP FRONT
2 PRINT

TOP FRONT   FIRST PRINT

BLACKBERRY VINE BORDER

43

FUCHSIA

The fuchsia pattern is easy to cut but hard to print because it requires much shading.

The baseline for this pattern should be drawn on the wall 6½ inches below where you wish the top of the design to fall. A corresponding line must also be drawn all the way across the first template, as indicated in the pattern in the book. The template is aligned on the wall by matching the lines. The fuchsia looks best without a background stripe or miniborder, for these might constrain its sensuous, flowing quality.

HEIGHT:

20 inches

NUMBER OF TEMPLATES:

Six

TIME:

3½ hours to transfer and cut; 40 minutes to print 3 feet.

SIZING TO FIT ROOM:

Repeats at 16½ inches as drawn; can be expanded to 19 inches.

COLORS

Use acrylics unless noted otherwise.

Hooker's Green
Raw Umber
Cadmium Yellow, Light
Acra Violet/Quinacridone Violet

Thalo Blue
Ultramarine Blue
Alizarin Crimson
White latex

BRUSHES:

One artist's rounded flat No. 8, three No. 10, and two No. 4 stencil brushes.

PRINTING:

Print 1—Print the stems in murky green that is a mixture of Hooker's Green and Raw Umber, using a No. 10 stencil brush.

Print 2—Print the leaves and additional stems in light bluish green, which is a mixture of Thalo Blue, white, and Cadmium Yellow, Light (Illus. 34).

Leaving template in place, paint transparent veins on leaves. Thin Hooker's Green until you have "green water." Load small amount of green water on a No. 8 rounded, flat artist's brush. Remove excess water with paper towel. Usually a touch to the towel is sufficient. Paint middle veins first, following the flow of the leaf shape. Then paint side veins, pulling brush from edge of leaf to middle vein. The veins should look organic, not stiff and geometric (Illus. 35). See color illustration of fuchsia border. Occasionally lift up template to check effect. You'll be surprised. It will look great!

Illus. 34. The second print of the fuchsia requires transparent veining in leaf shapes. The first step is to print the shapes all one color, light blue-green. Note the baseline markings on template.

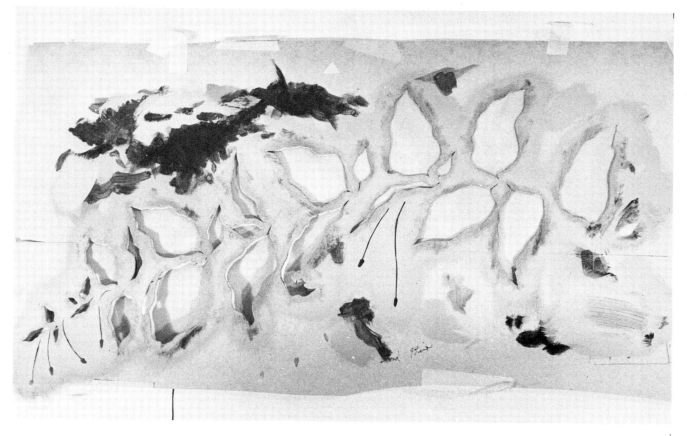

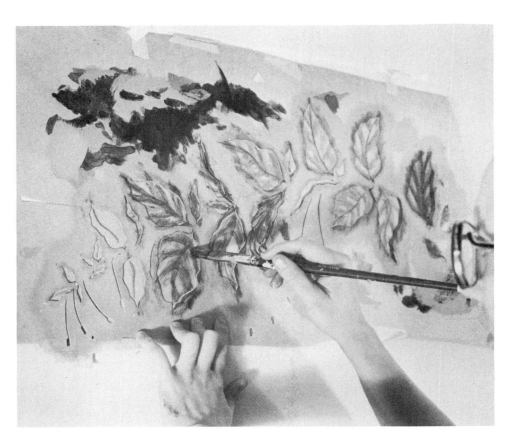

Illus. 35.   With moist brush, paint in center vein. Be sure to follow the flow of the leaf. Then pull in side veins to meet the center vein. Pull from edge of template towards middle.

Print 3—The delicate stamens are printed in Acra Violet with a No. 4 stencil brush.

Print 4—For fuchsia petticoats, prepare palette with several pinks and purples mixed from Acra Violet with white and Alizarin Crimson with Ultramarine Blue. Load two No. 10 stencil brushes with two of the colors. As the brushes run dry, load on other pinks and purples. Alternate the colors in a random fashion as you print; don't print them all in a line in one color. When the base colors are done, take a No. 4 brush to stipple darker pink or darker purple colors onto blossoms and use the dry-brush technique described in the Special Effects section.

Print 5—Use Acra Violet mixed with white on a No. 10 stencil brush to print fuchsia overskirts. These can be darker or lighter than the petticoat petals. If you want them very light, however, you must first print them in white, and then, leaving template in place, print them in the light color. Otherwise, the darker color underneath will show through. Highlight tops and upward curves of petals with a pounce of dry-brush white: dip a No. 4 stencil brush in white and then dry off most of the paint on a paper towel so that the brush makes white speckles when pounced on petals.

Print 6—The unopened fuchsia buds are light yellow-green with a hint of pink on the tips of the larger buds. Mix yellow-green from Cadmium Yellow, Light, Hooker's Green, and white. Print with a No. 10 stencil brush. Make pink highlight color from the pink of the flower overskirts lightened with additional white. Apply with a No. 4 stencil brush.

46

|1 |2 |3 |4 |5 |6 |7

FIRST PRINT

PART A

circle registration
for pattern assembly only
do not cut out

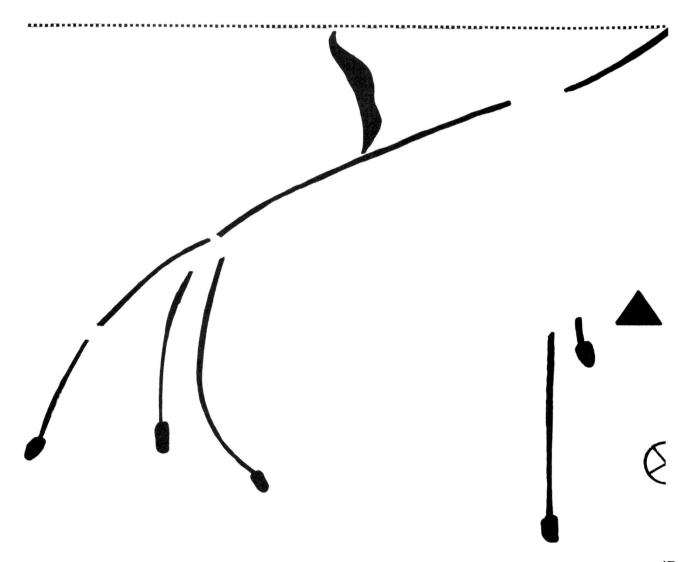

FIRST PRINT
PART B

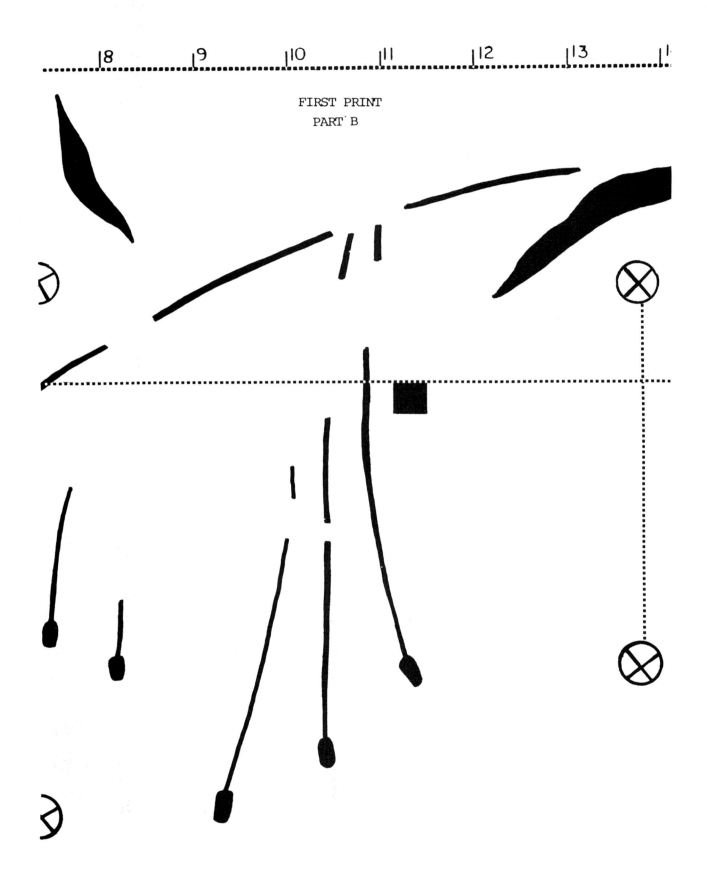

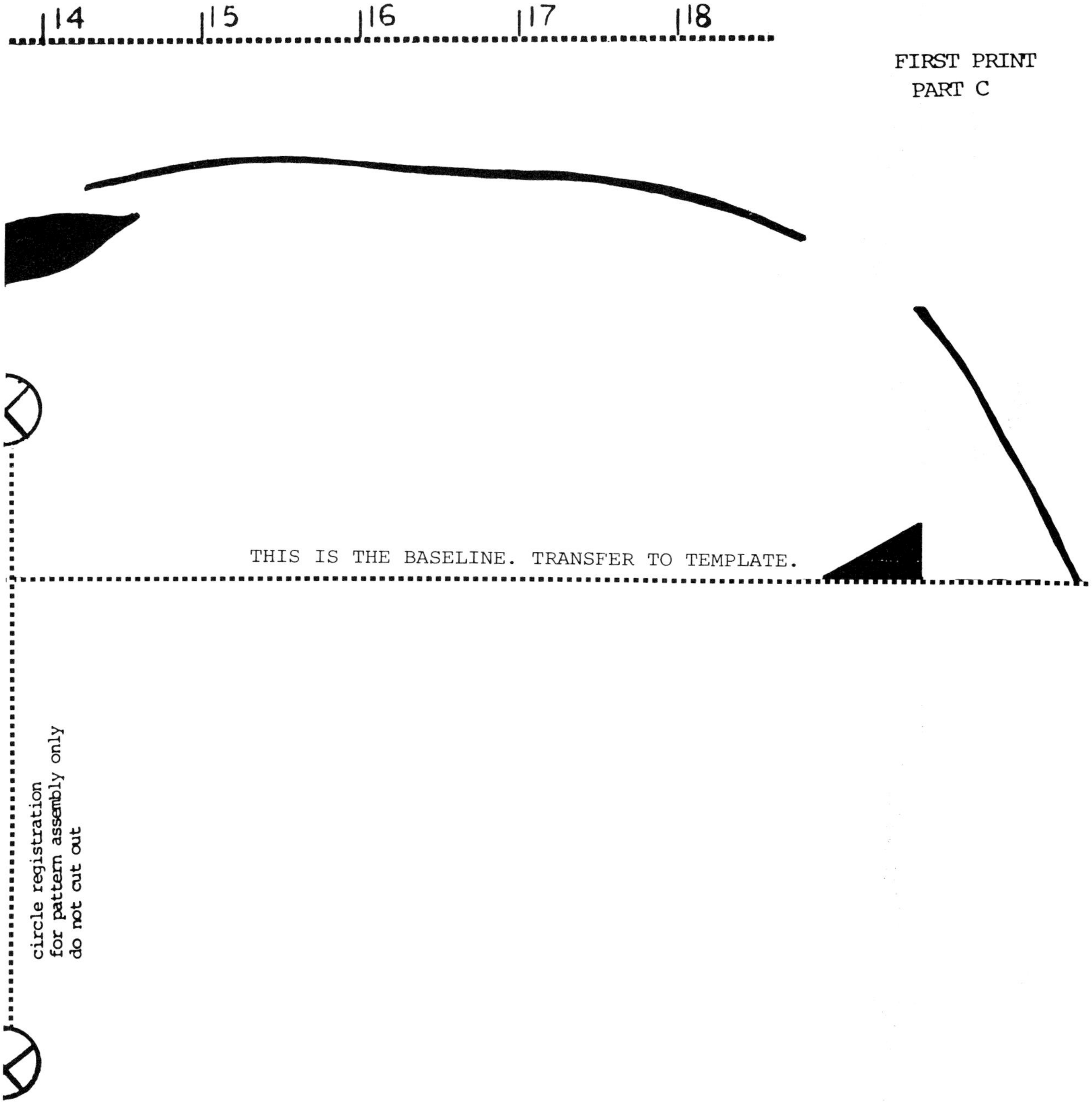

FIRST PRINT
PART C

THIS IS THE BASELINE. TRANSFER TO TEMPLATE.

circle registration
for pattern assembly only
do not cut out

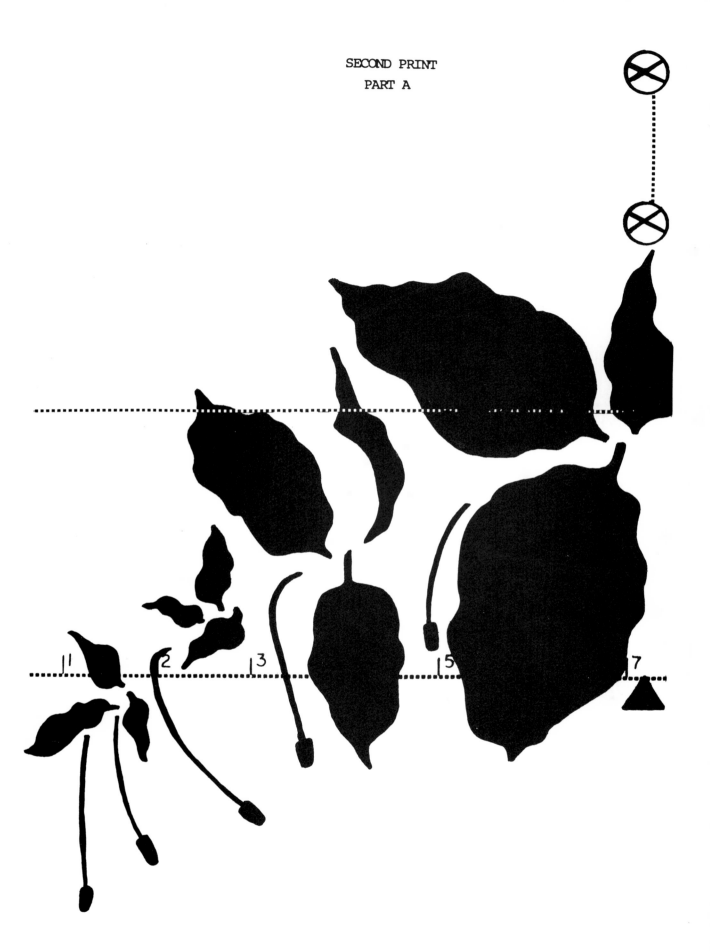

SECOND PRINT

PART B

circle registration
for pattern assembly only
do not cut out

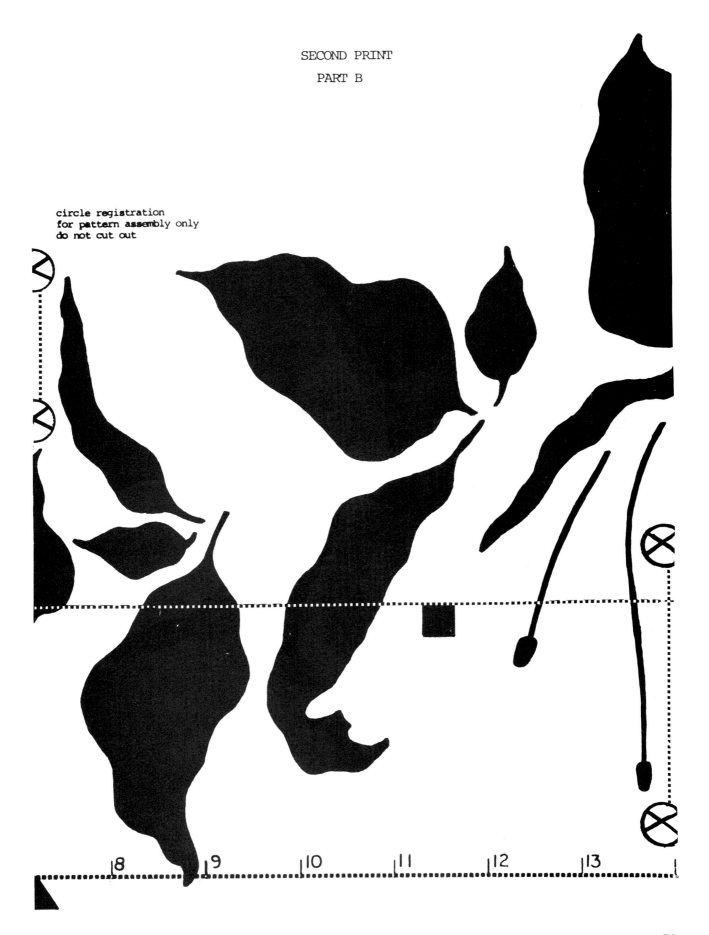

8   9   10   11   12   13

51

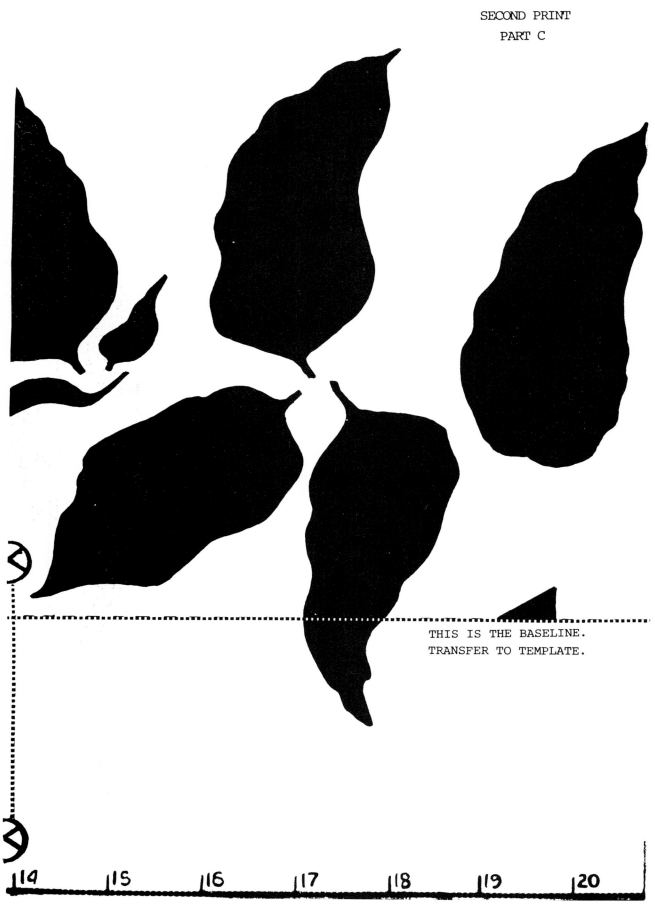

THIS IS THE BASELINE.
TRANSFER TO TEMPLATE.

|14 |15 |16 |17 |18 |19 |20

THIRD PRINT

PART A

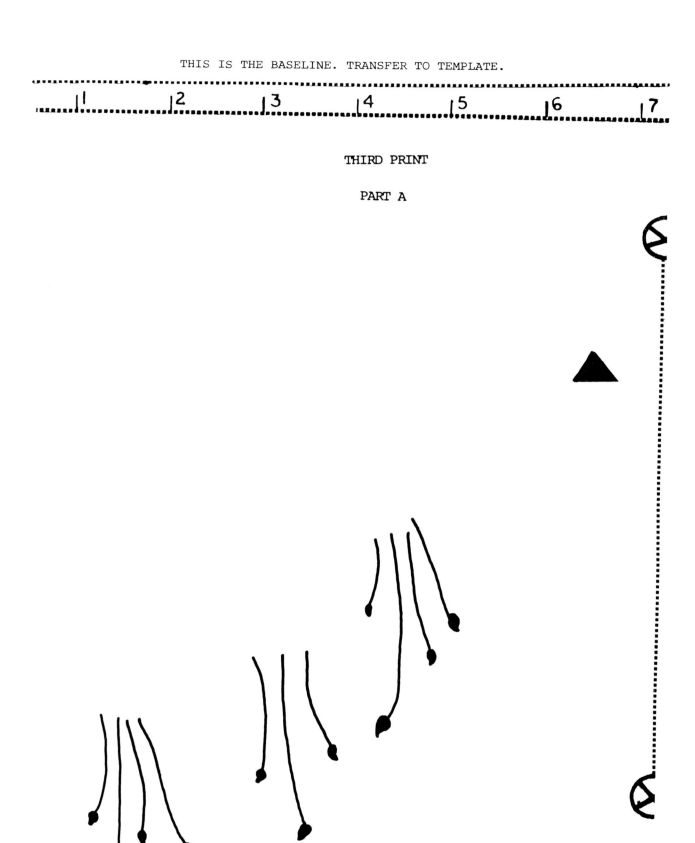

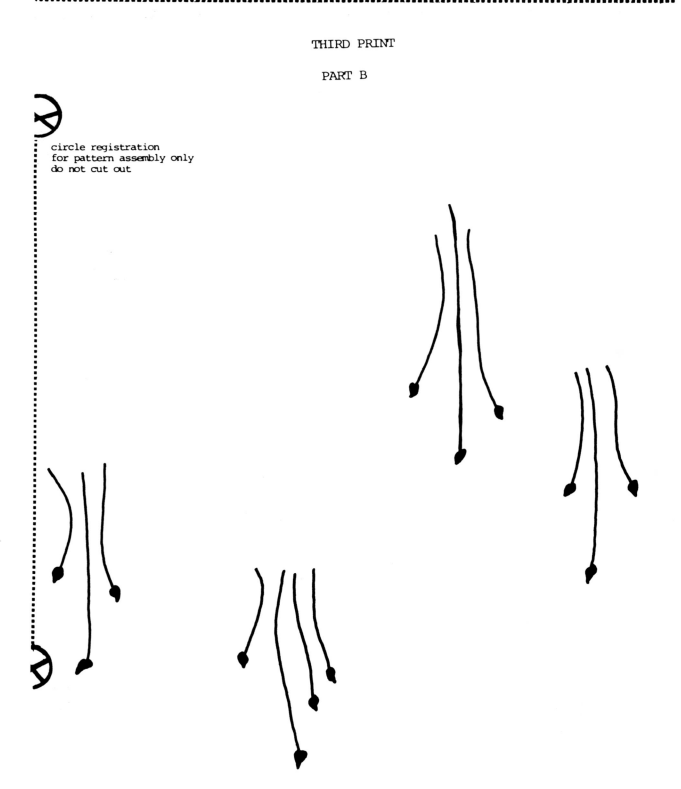

THIRD PRINT

PART B

circle registration
for pattern assembly only
do not cut out

1 2 3 4 5 6

circle registration
for pattern assembly
do not cut out

THIS IS THE BASELINE. TRANSFER TO TEMPLATE.

|7 |8 |9 |10 |11 |12 |13

FIFTH PRINT
PART A

THIS IS THE BASELINE. TRANSFER TO TEMPLATE.

|1 |2 |3 |4 |5 |6

circle registration
for pattern assembly only
do not cut out

57

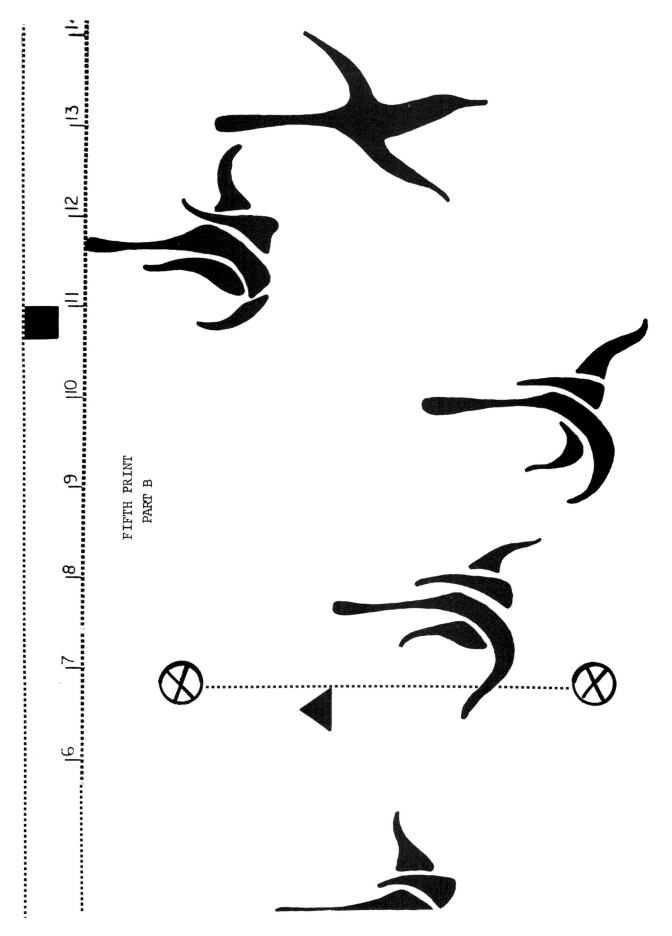

FIFTH PRINT
PART B

58

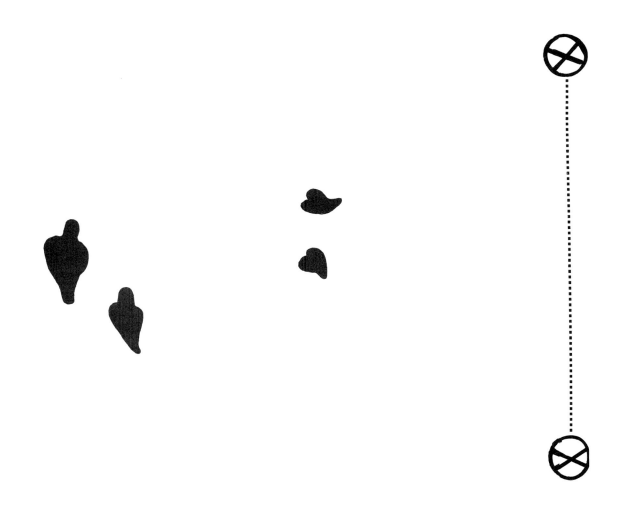

SIXTH PRINT
PART A

|7 |8 |9 |10 |11 |12 |13

THIS IS THE BASELINE. TRANSFER TO TEMPLATE.

SIXTH PRINT

PART B

circle registration
for pattern assembly
do not cut out

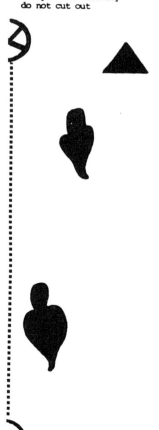

60

FERN

The fern border has been designed to be flexible, and anyone can expect a good result. This is the easiest design to print, since the fronds are positioned at random, eliminating the need for baselines and registration marks. It is not, however, an easy border to cut because of the wavy margins of the fronds. The ferns are intended as a base border, along the floor, but also would look good as a low wainscoting—about 18 to 19 inches off the floor. If used as wainscoting, print the ferns a little shorter. The fern border would be fabulous, of course, with wicker furniture and real plants, creating a tropical mood. It looks good growing out of the arched miniborder.

SPECIAL TIPS:

Because of the ruffly edges of the fronds, this design is best made from Mylar, which is easier to cut. Leave at least a 1-inch frame of solid Mylar around the cutout images.

HEIGHT:

If you use all the fronds the height is 18 to 20 inches. But you can narrow the border by not printing the bottoms of the taller fronds. However, they will look funny if printed less than 13 inches tall.

NUMBER OF TEMPLATES:

Eight

TIME:

2.5 to 3 hours to transfer and cut; approximately 20 minutes to print 3 feet of border (depending on density of ferns).

COLORS

Use acrylics unless noted otherwise.

Hooker's Green   Ultramarine Blue
Cadmium Yellow, Light   White (latex house paint)
Raw Umber

BRUSHES:

Two No. 6 or larger stencil brushes. If you use the largest stencil brush—No. 10—it will speed the work.

PRINTING:

First print a row of background fronds, then overlay them with a border of darker foreground fronds. The background fronds should be lighter and bluer to give the illusion of depth.

To print background fronds: The background is composed of the larger fronds. Cover the wall fairly evenly with them, without much overlap, but leave occasional small gaps into which small curled foreground fronds in the "fiddle" stage will be inserted later. Print the fronds vertically, or at an angle. They need not go all the way down to the baseline. The foreground ferns will do that.

Mix Hooker's Green, a bit of Cadmium Yellow, Light, and white to make light yellow-green. Then mix a second batch of paint from Hooker's Green, Ultramarine Blue and a small amount of Raw Umber to make a light blue-green. Load the brush first with one color and paint that out. Then load the brush with the other. You can sometimes load it twice in a row with the same color.

To print foreground fronds, prepare the palette with a dollop of Hooker's Green mixed with a tiny bit of white and another dollop of Ultramarine Blue mixed with Raw Umber. As with the background fronds, use one color for a while and then switch to the other.

The foreground fronds are much darker than those behind them. These are the fronds the eye will notice most, so they must be dynamically organized upon the wall. Keep them from overlapping as this results in a knotted, tangled look that is more like bones than ferns. Print smaller curled fronds in open areas. To create shorter ferns, print just the top portion of a template. The foreground ferns are printed right down to the baseline.

For double the number of fern templates, cut out all the fronds a second time in reverse—as mirror images of the original templates.

OTHER IDEAS:

Scumble a background halfway up the wall behind the ferns, ending no more than 8 inches up from the baseline. To scumble, mix a green that is lighter than the lightest green used to print the ferns. Then scribble with your stencil brush or a No. 10 artist's brush (flat or round). All of the scumbled area will be covered with paint, but some areas more so than others, producing a mottled effect. The top edge of the scumbled border should be fuzzy (Illus. 36).

The ferns don't have to be printed in green. They would look wonderful in different pinks or in shades of grey.

Illus. 36. To scumble background use large artists' or stencil brush to very randomly apply light coating of color. Don't go up too far—6 to 8 inches up from baseline looks best. It is even more interesting to have two colors scumbled together.

PART A

PART B

circle registration
for pattern assembly only
do not cut out

65

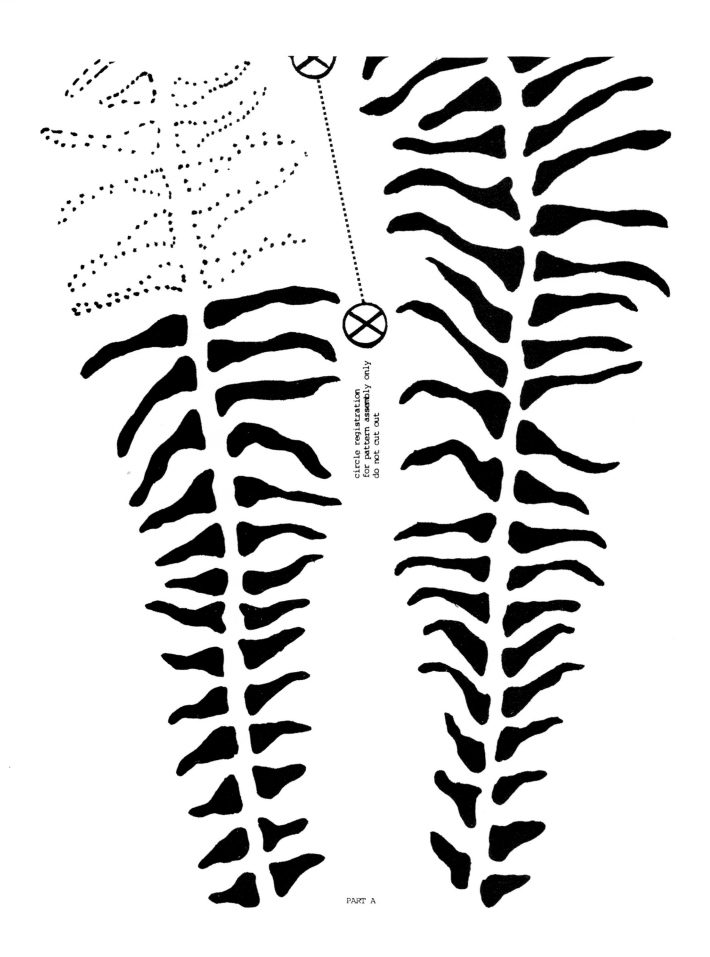

circle registration
for pattern assembly only
do not cut out

PART A

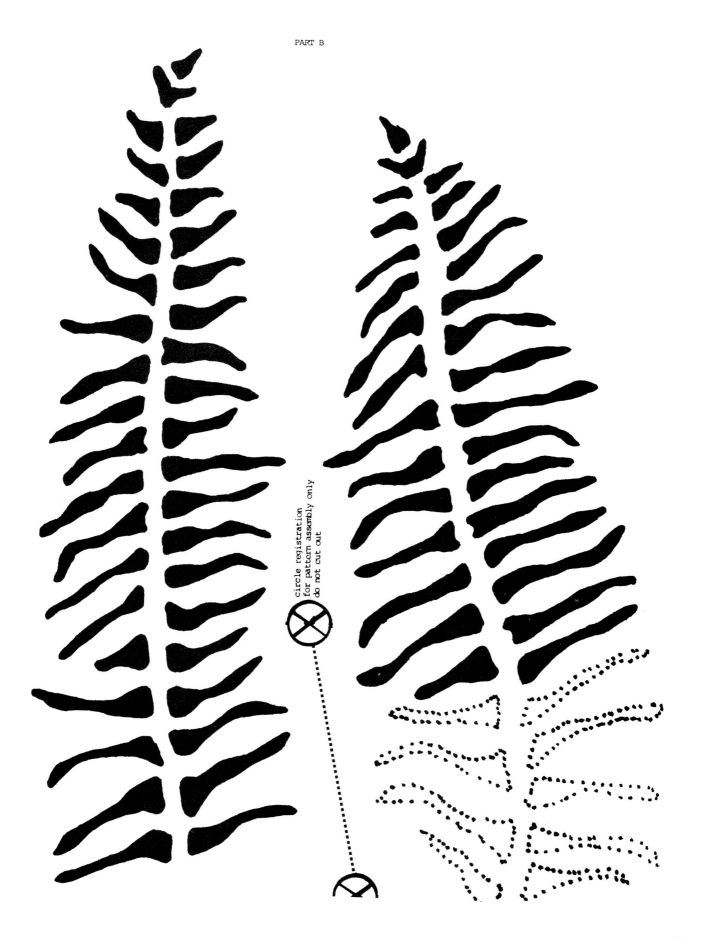

circle registration
for pattern assembly only
do not cut out

PART C

CALLA LILY

Fans of calla lilies can be printed pink on a pale lavender background, white on a pink background, or as pictured in the color section. White calla lilies need a background in a medium value to show well, with the blossoms printed twice for a distinct print. The calla lilies look good with the Art Deco miniborder.

HEIGHT:

10 inches

NUMBER OF TEMPLATES:

Five

TIME:

2½ hours to transfer and cut; 25 minutes to print 3 feet of the complete design.

SIZING TO FIT ROOM:

Repeats every 11 inches. Size to fit room by inserting random element, a leaf, which is 2 inches wide.

COLORS

Use acrylics unless noted otherwise.

Hooker's Green　　　　　　　　Naphthol Crimson

Cadmium Yellow, Light　　　　Acra Violet/Quinacridone Violet

Ultramarine Blue　　　　　　　Yellow Orange AZO

Raw Umber·　　　　　　　　　White latex

BRUSHES:

One No. 2, one No. 4, and two No. 10 stencil brushes.

PRINTING:

Print 1—The first print (leaves) does not rest on the baseline. Since the second template does, put the second template over the first and mark where stems end. Draw a straight line connecting the stem ends across the entire template. Match the pencilled line to baseline on the wall as you print.

Print the leaves with a No. 10 stencil brush in a dark green mixed from Hooker's Green, Cadmium Yellow, Light, and a bit of white. Vary the color slightly from leaf to leaf, making the upper left leaf more yellow so it appears to catch the sunlight.

Then, leaving the template in place, dry-brush shade the two bottom leaves with a No. 4 brush dipped in a dark blue-green made from Hooker's Green mixed with Ultramarine Blue (Illus. 37). The idea is to make the leaves appear ruffly. The leaves have slightly wavy margins. Stripe them with a vague wiggly V horizontally, like chevron stripes, running the line between two places where the leaf narrows, using a No. 2 stencil brush for the small veins (Illus. 38). Refer to section on Special Effects for more information about dry-brush shading.

Also, shade the lower edges of leaves.

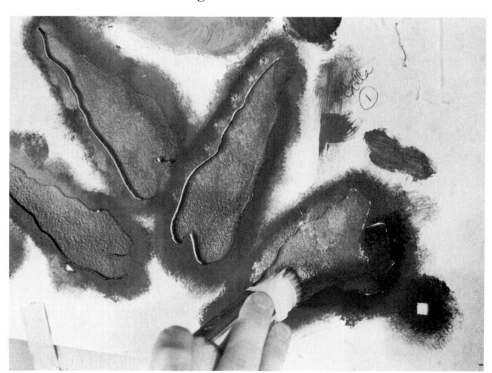

Illus. 37.　Shading of lower edges of two bottom leaves is accomplished by dry-brush soft shading with a #4 stencil brush.

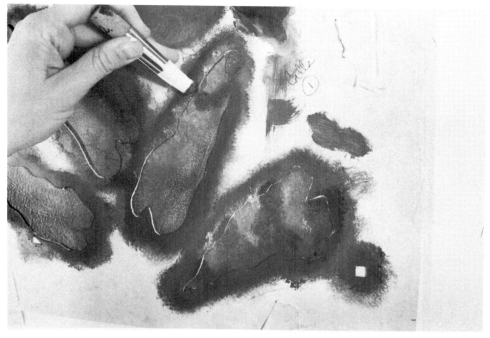

Illus. 38. Small v-shaped veins are stippled into ripples for all leaves with a #2 stencil brush.

Print 2—Add white and Cadmium Yellow, Light to the leaf color and print the stems, except the middle one, in this yellower, lighter green. For the middle stem, add more white to stem color so it stands out where it crosses the leaf. The leaf edge in lower left of the template also needs special treatment. Add blue and white to stem color, load brush, wipe off most of the paint on a paper towel, and then, with a very dry brush, paint just the top edge of the leaf, blending paint towards the bottom edge. Use a No. 10 stencil brush for all parts of print 2.

Print 3—Print lilies in light mauve—a mixture of Raw Umber, Naphthol Crimson, white, and a small amount of Acra Violet. Use a No. 10 stencil brush.

Print 4—For lily shadows, combine paint as for blossoms but use less white and more Raw Umber to produce a darker mixture. Apply with a No. 10 stencil brush.

Print 5—Using a clean and dry No. 2 stencil brush, underprint stamens with white then with Yellow Orange AZO.

RANDOM
ELEMENT
CALLA
LILY

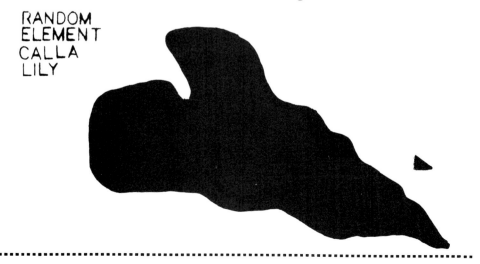

FIRST PRINT
PART A

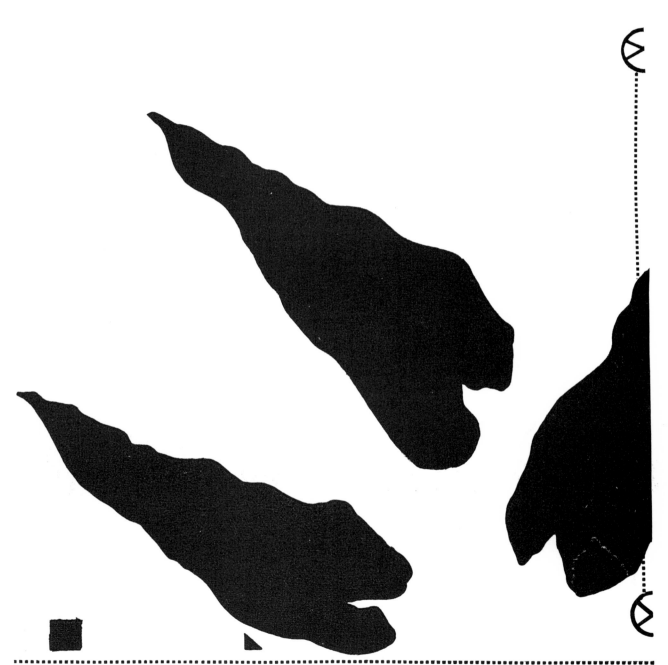

THIS IS THE BASELINE. TRANSFER TO TEMPLATE.

FIRST PRINT
PART B

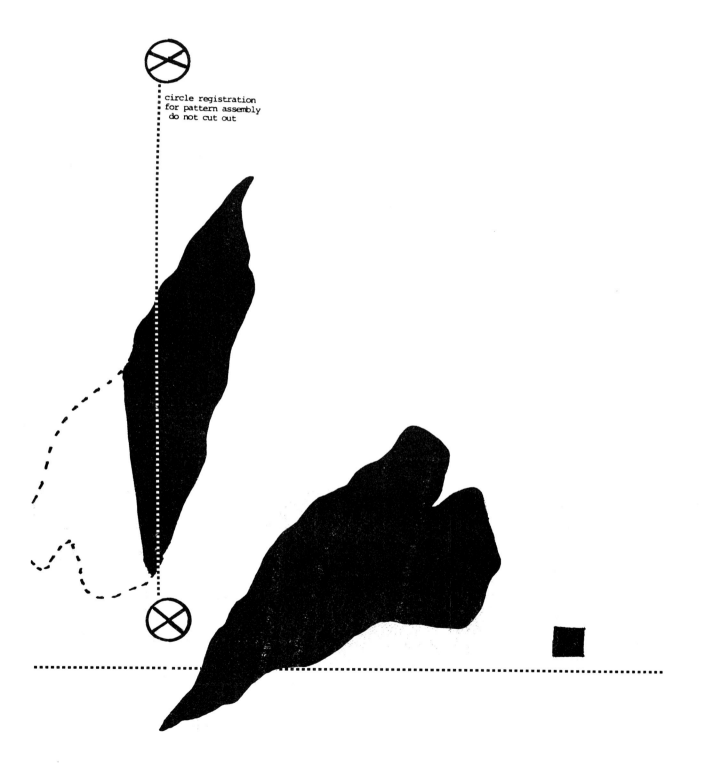

circle registration
for pattern assembly
do not cut out

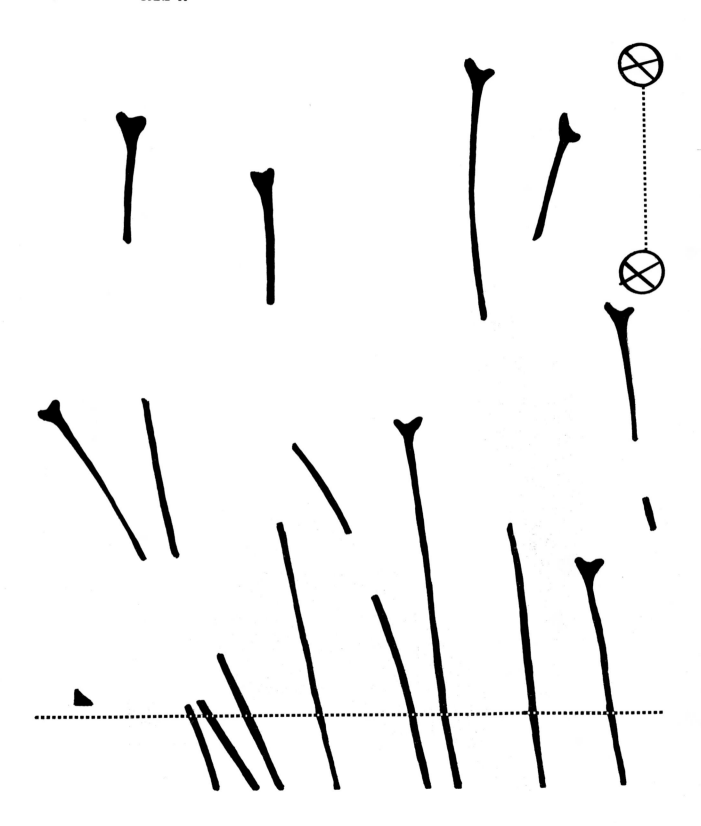

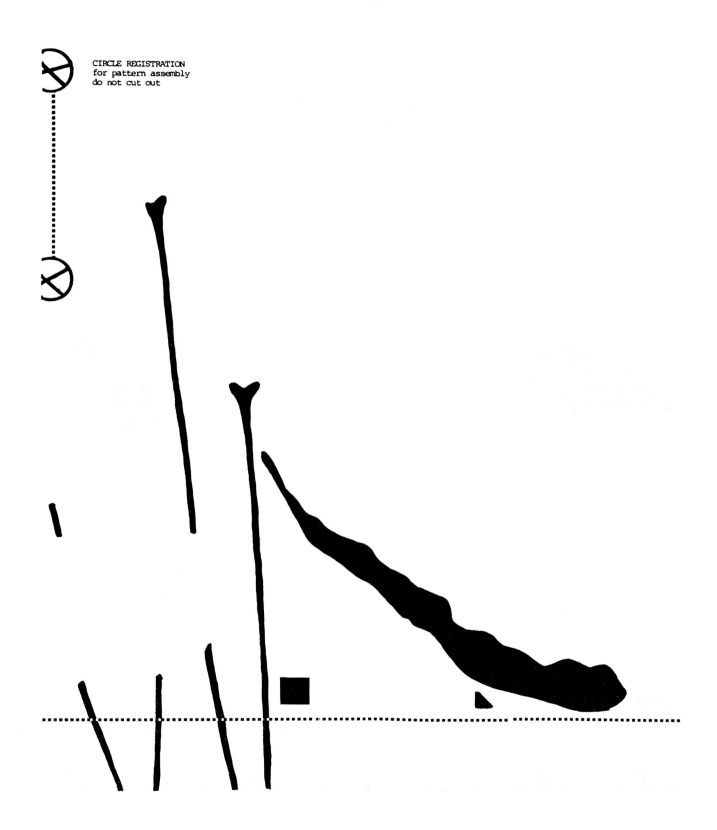

CIRCLE REGISTRATION
for pattern assembly
do not cut out

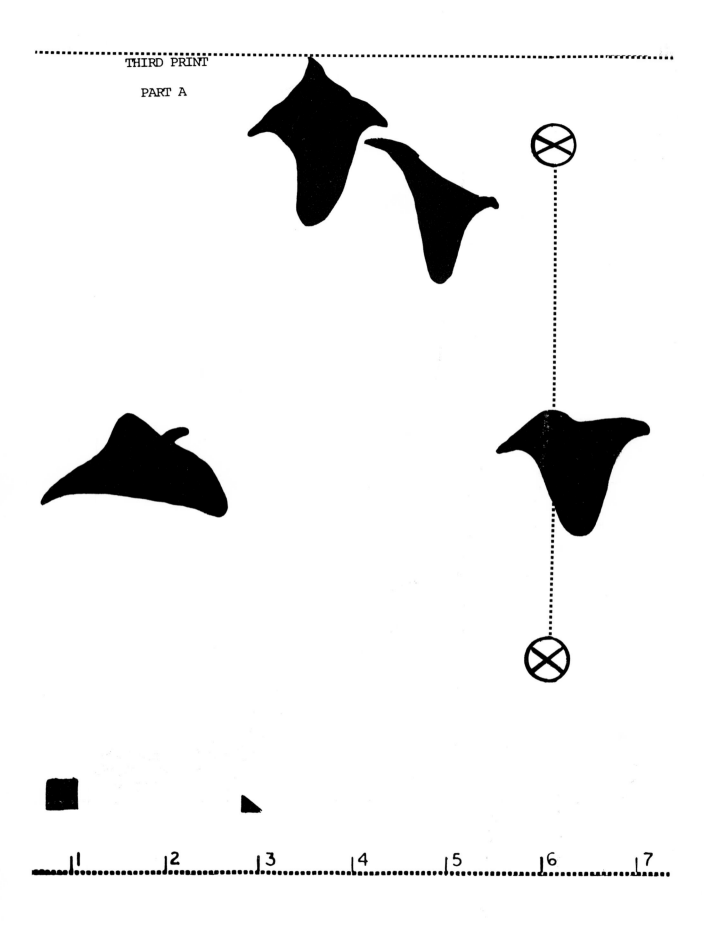

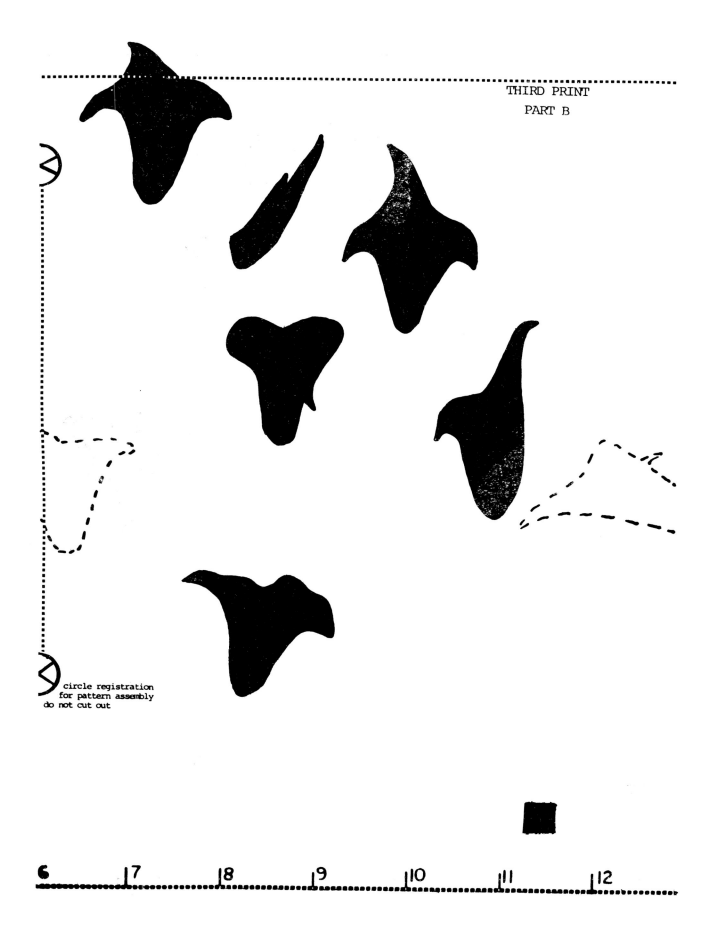

circle registration
for pattern assembly
do not cut out

6   7   8   9   10   11   12

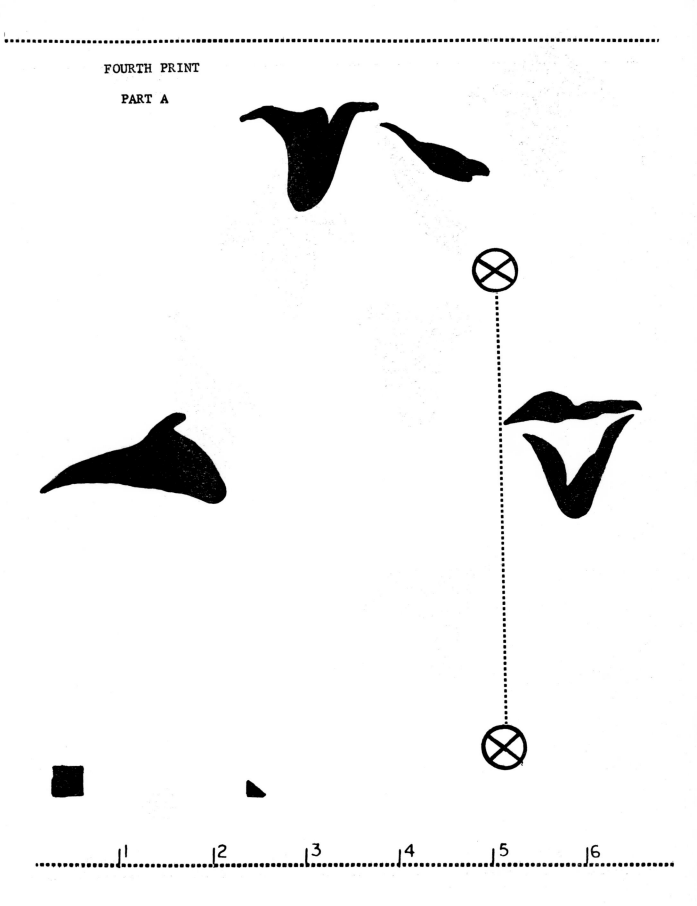

FOURTH PRINT

PART A

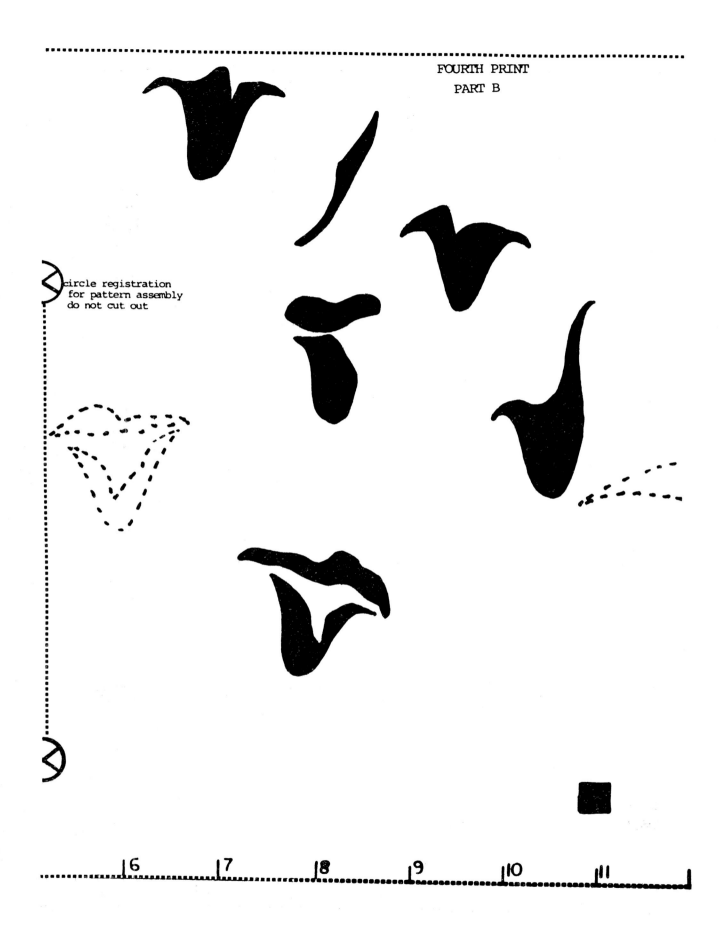

circle registration
for pattern assembly
do not cut out

6   7   8   9   10   11

79

PART A

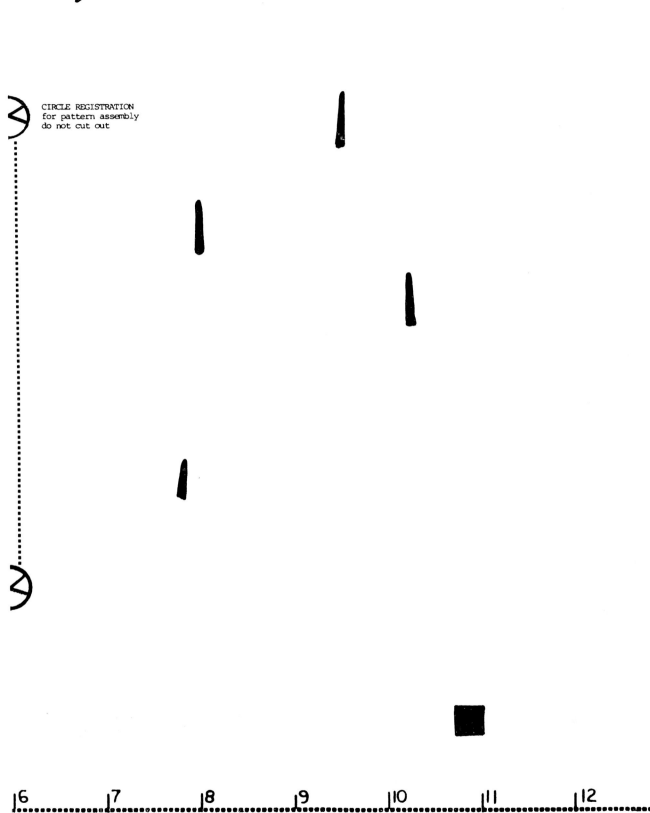

FIFTH PRINT   PART B

CIRCLE REGISTRATION
for pattern assembly
do not cut out

6   7   8   9   10   11   12

81

FORGET-ME-NOT

HEIGHT:
   10 inches

NUMBER OF TEMPLATES:
   Three, plus three small ones for random element

TIME:
   2½ hours to transfer and cut; 30 minutes to print a 3-foot section with complete image.

SIZING TO FIT ROOM:
   As drawn, design repeats every 11¼ inches and can be expanded as large as 11¾ inches. Additional gaps can be filled with the random element—a sprig of the plant that requires about 3 inches to print.

COLORS
   Use acrylics unless noted otherwise.

Chromium Oxide Green	Ultramarine Blue
Thalo Blue	Hooker's Green
Cadmium Yellow, Light	White latex

BRUSHES:

Two No. 10 stencil brushes and one No. 2 artist's round (this is not a stencil brush).

PRINTING:

Print 1—The first template does not print to the bottom edge of the image. To compensate, fit the second template (print 2—the stems) on top of the first template (print 1—the leaves). Then, with a pencil, mark the bottom points of all the stems. Now there are little pencil marks on the first template where the stems end. Using a straightedge, draw a straight line through all the pencil marks. Use this line to align the template as you print, as discussed under Printing.

Print 1—The leaves are printed by loading two colors on one brush for a mottled effect. First, mix Hooker's Green and Cadmium Yellow, Light with a bit of white on your palette to produce a light yellow-green. Then mix Ultramarine Blue, Raw Umber and Chromium Oxide Green with a bit of white to make a brownish blue-green. Alternately load the brush with the yellow-green mixture on one side and the white on the other or the brownish blue-green mixture on one side and again white on the other. Don't clean the brush between these alternations (Illus. 39). The white stays constant—it is always loaded on the same side of the brush. Alternate the other colors. Stipple the paint into the template, skipping around, so that about half the leaves are painted when the brush is in its yellow-green and white phase, and half receive the brownish blue-green treatment. See Special Effects for more on mottling.

Print 2—The stems are painted Hooker's Green.

Print 3—Mix Thalo Blue with white on palette for the flowers. Sometimes mix a little more white with the blue, sometimes less, to

Illus. 39.   The mottled effect for the forget-me-not leaves is achieved by loading the brush with two different greens and printing. Notice darker color on right and lighter on left.

83

achieve a slight variation in color (Illus. 40). For additional shading, with the template still in place and using the same brush, dip the brush in straight Ultramarine Blue and pounce it on paper towels until brush is nearly dry. It should produce dots when pounced. Apply one pounce of dots to each cluster of flowers. See Special Effects for additional instruction on speckling.

Make flower centers by loading No. 2 artist's brush with white, then dotting the middle of the flowers.

Illus. 40. Mottled printing of blue flowers in the third printing is the background for dry brushing darker blue flecks on top.

The three templates that compose the random element are printed just like the larger design (Illus. 41).

Illus. 41. Print random element templates as you print others. Printing at the same time assures a consistent paint color variation.

Other Ideas

Forget-me-nots are not always blue. They can be pink—use Alizarin Crimson with white and a bit of Raw Umber. Middles can be yellow. Or make them purple with yellow cores.

FIRST PRINT
PART A

THIS IS THE BASELINE. TRANSFER TO TEMPLATE.

circle registration
for pattern assembly only
do not cut out

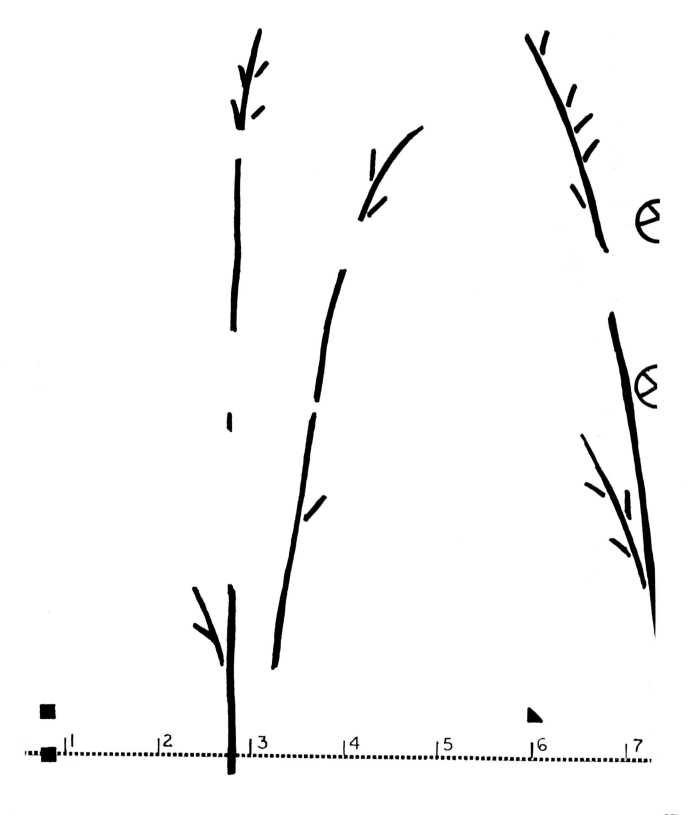

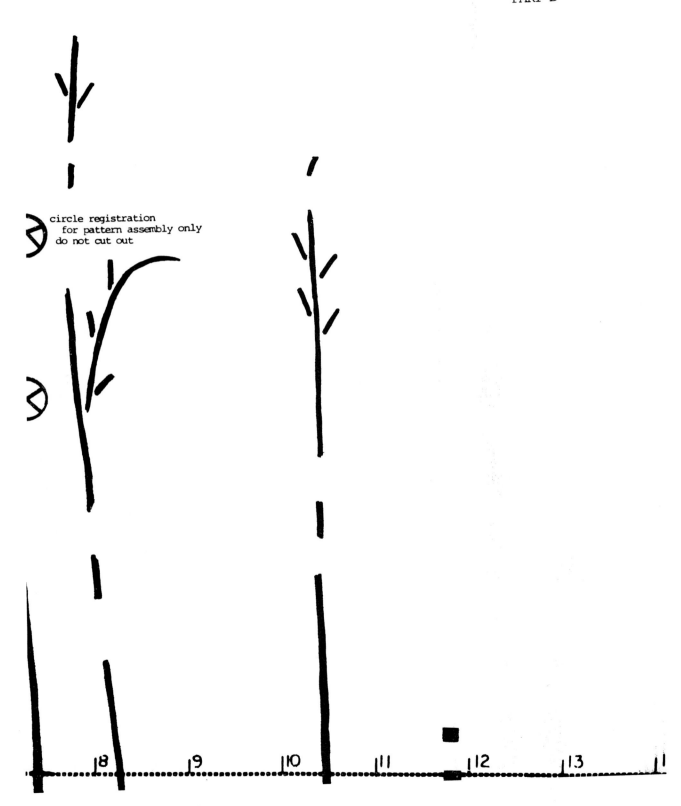

circle registration
for pattern assembly only
do not cut out

THIRD PRINT
PART A

|1 |2 |3 |4 |5 |6

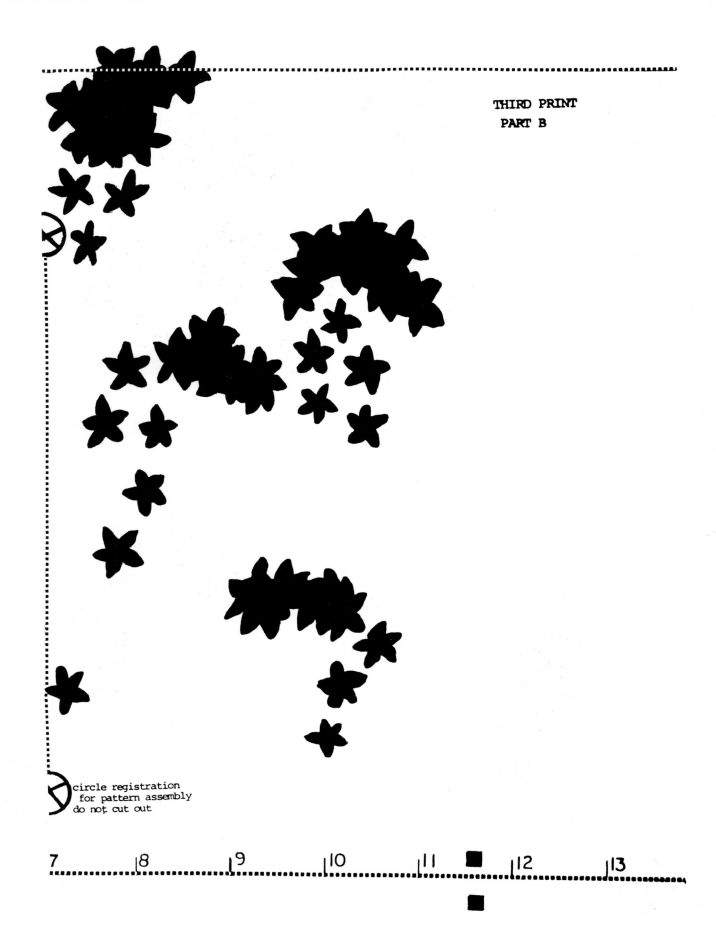

THIRD PRINT
PART B

circle registration
for pattern assembly
do not cut out

7   8   9   10   11   12   13

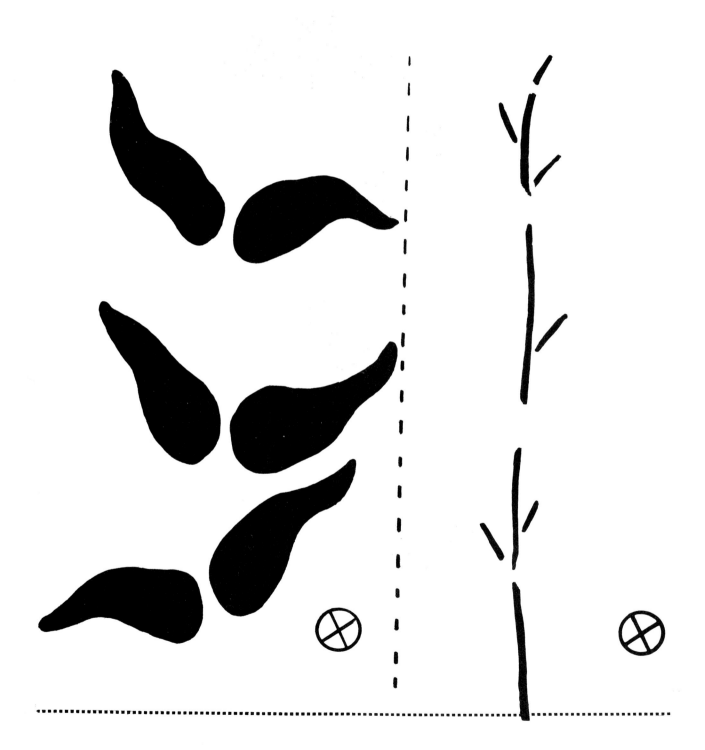

FORGET-ME-NOT
RANDOM
ELEMENT

SECOND PRINT

FIRST PRINT

FORGET - ME-NOT
RANDOM
ELEMENT

THIRD PRINT

BEGONIA

The calligraphic qualities of the begonia border would complement an Oriental interior. The design looks best printed on a background stripe of yellow or light green, without a miniborder. A leaf-shading technique enhances the foliage.

HEIGHT:

6 inches

NUMBER OF TEMPLATES:

Four—stems, leaves, stems/blossoms, blossoms/scales

TIME:

2½ hours to transfer and cut; 25 minutes to print a 3-foot section with complete image.

SIZING TO FIT ROOM:

As drawn, pattern repeats every 28 inches. Expand it up to 29¾ inches. The design uses two complete begonia stems. Either half of the design—either stem—can be printed separately as a random element. The right begonia stem fills from 10 to 12 inches (depending upon how much you tuck its stem under the begonia next to it); the left begonia stem fills 20½ inches.

COLORS

Use acrylics unless noted otherwise.

Burnt Umber   Hooker's Green
Dioxazine Violet   Yellow Oxide/Yellow Ochre
Cadmium Red, Medium   White latex
Brilliant Yellow

BRUSHES:

Three No. 10 and one No. 6 stencil brushes.

PRINTING:

Print 1—Stems are dark yellow-green. Prepare by mixing Hooker's Green, Yellow Oxide, and a small amount of white for opacity. Use a No. 10 stencil brush.

Print 2—Print the leaves twice. First apply a basic coat of murky dark-green made from mixing Hooker's Green, Yellow Oxide, Burnt Umber (medium value), and a bit of white. Print all shapes with an even layer of color, using a No. 10 stencil brush.

Without moving the template, shade the leaves brownish purple by mixing Dioxazine Violet and Burnt Umber with a few drops of white for opacity. Try to keep it from reading either purple or brown. As you mix the color, be ready to adjust it when you see how it prints. Apply the brownish purple with an extremely dry No. 10 stencil brush by wiping the loaded brush on paper towels until the paint is almost entirely removed. Then, working with a light stippling stroke, shade the leaves along their edges, or perhaps just along their lower edges. Do not shade the stems; leave them green.

Print 3—Blossoms, stems, and a leaf are all on this template. First, print the blossoms a medium salmon by mixing Cadmium Red, Medium, Brilliant Yellow, and white, using a No. 10 stencil brush. After printing the blossoms—without moving the template—wipe as much paint as possible off the blossom brush with a paper towel. Then dip the brush lightly into white and pounce a bit of white onto the blossoms to speckle them. This makes them appear to glisten.

Still leaving the template in place and using the No. 10 stencil brush, print the leaves and stems in a slightly darker shade of the brownish purple that was used to shade the first set of leaves. The large leaf on this template gets a special treatment: Print it as you did the leaves on the second template, applying an undercoat of murky green and then shading with a dry brush of brownish purple. But, make this leaf slightly darker than the other leaves to give the illusion of depth.

The fourth template is used to print the outer petals of the blossoms and the paper scales found in the joints of begonia stems. Using a No. 10 stencil brush, print the outer petals with the light salmon color (more white added to the original blossom color). As with the first blossom print, speckle the outer petals with a white dry brush. Print scales with a No. 6 stencil brush, using the flower color that has been toned down with Burnt Umber.

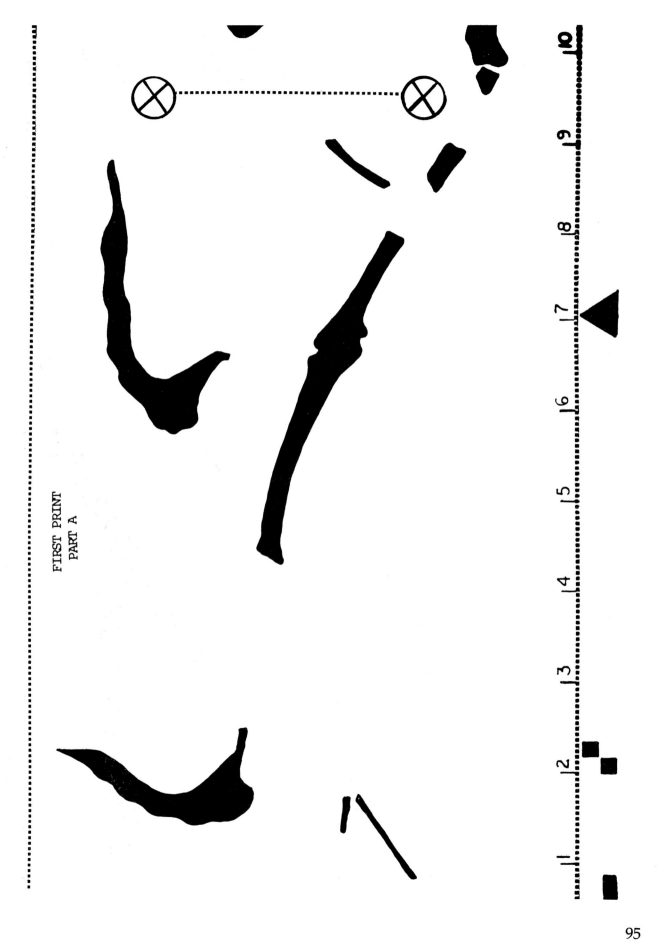

FIRST PRINT
PART A

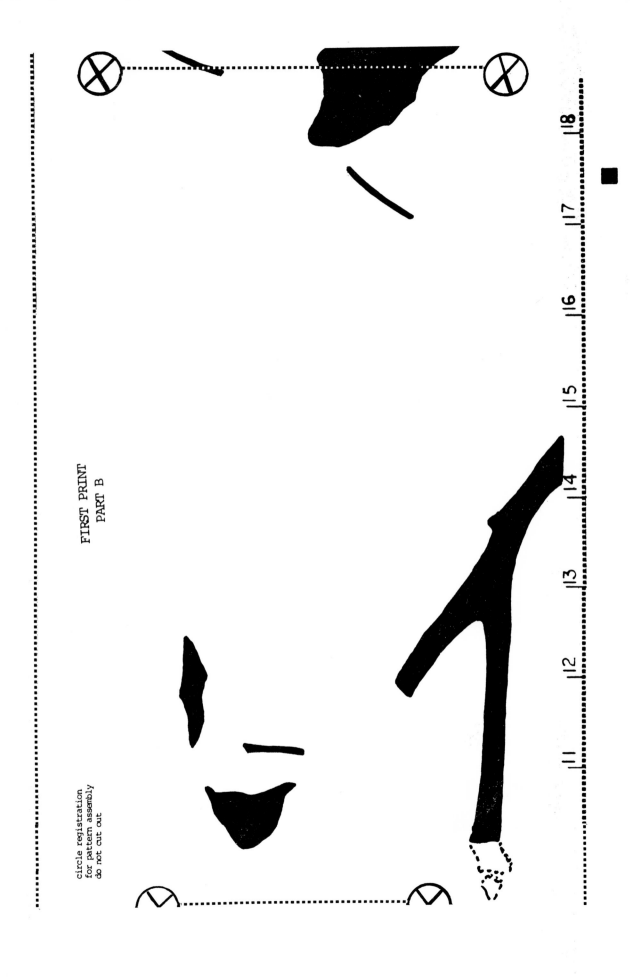

FIRST PRINT
PART B

circle registration
for pattern assembly
do not cut out

18 17 16 15 14 13 12 11

96

FIRST PRINT
PART C

CIRCLE REGISTRATION
for pattern assembly
do not cut out

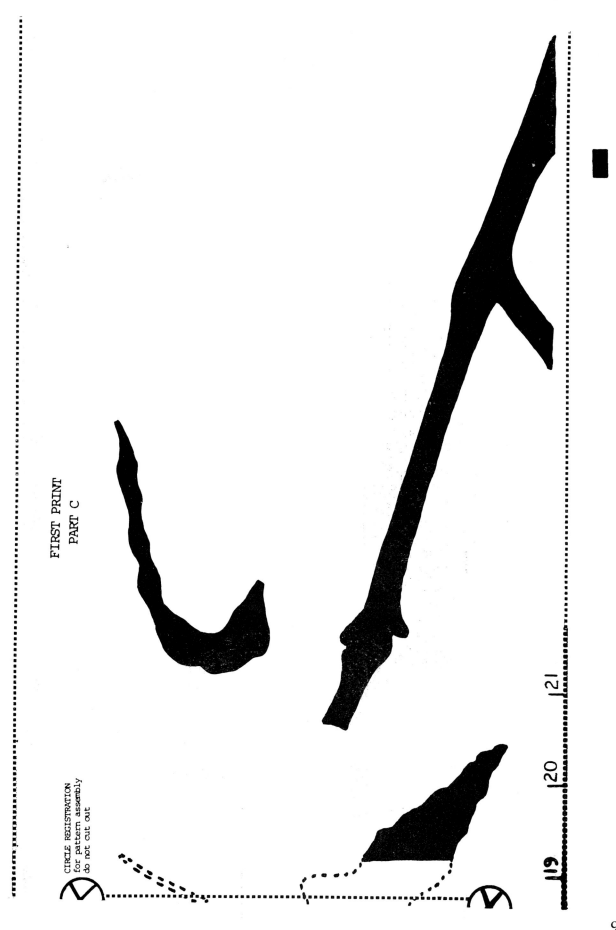

|19 |20 |21

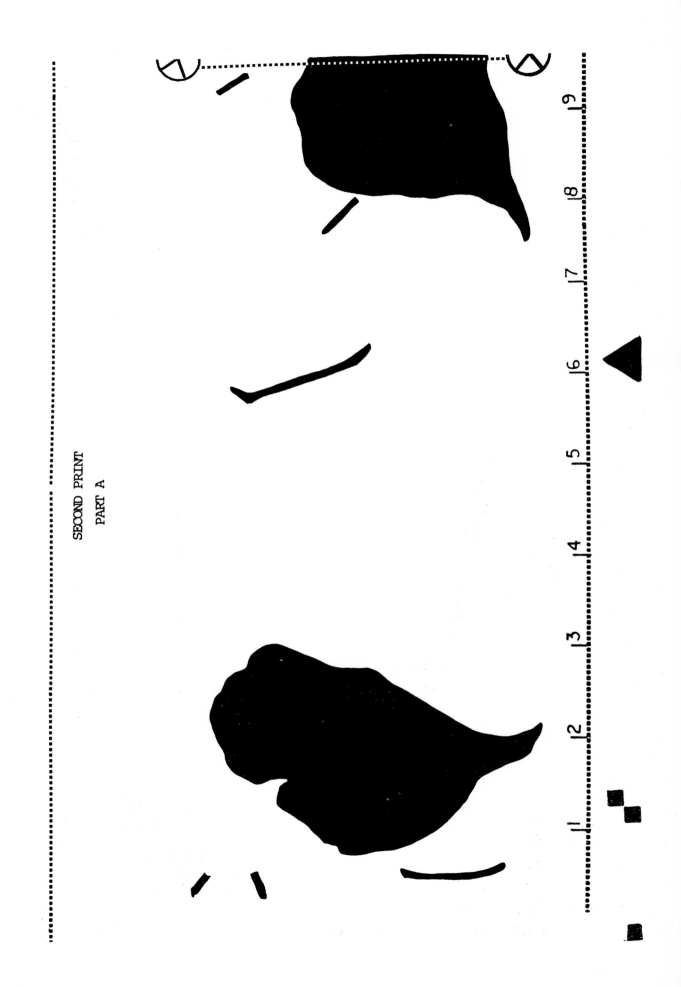

SECOND PRINT

PART A

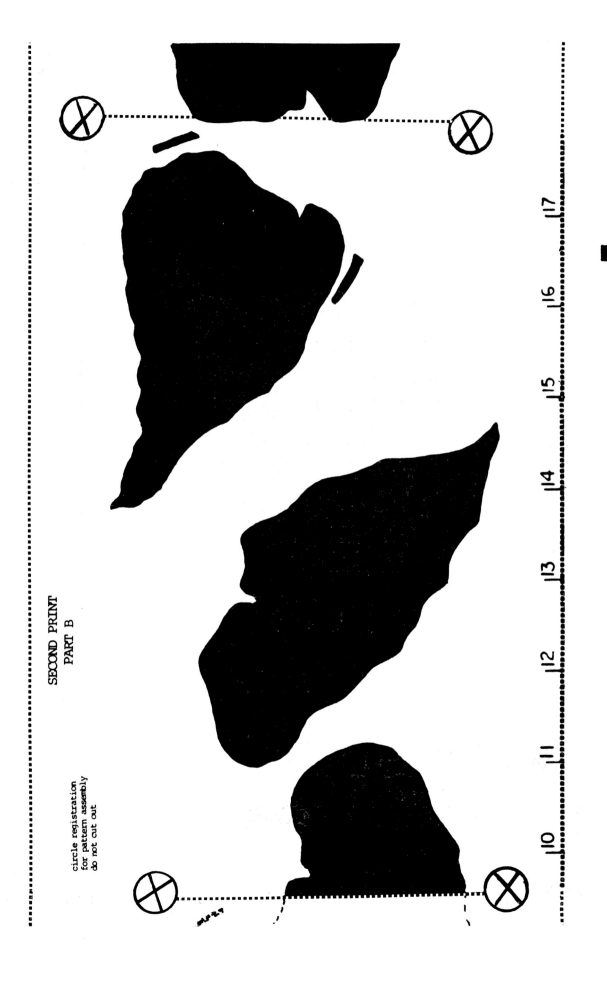

SECOND PRINT
PART B

circle registration
for pattern assembly
do not cut out

10   11   12   13   14   15   16   17

99

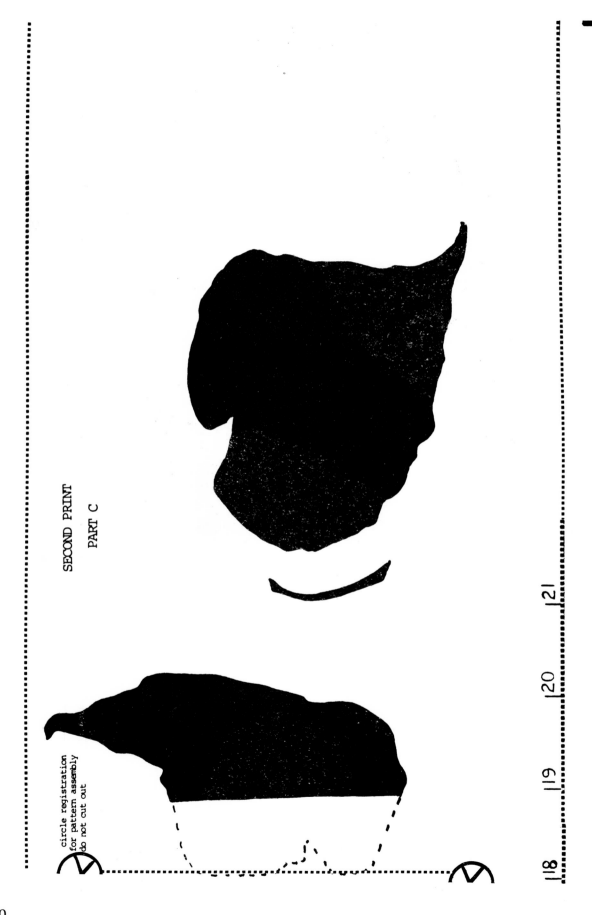

SECOND PRINT

PART C

circle registration
for pattern assembly
do not cut out

|18 |19 |20 |21

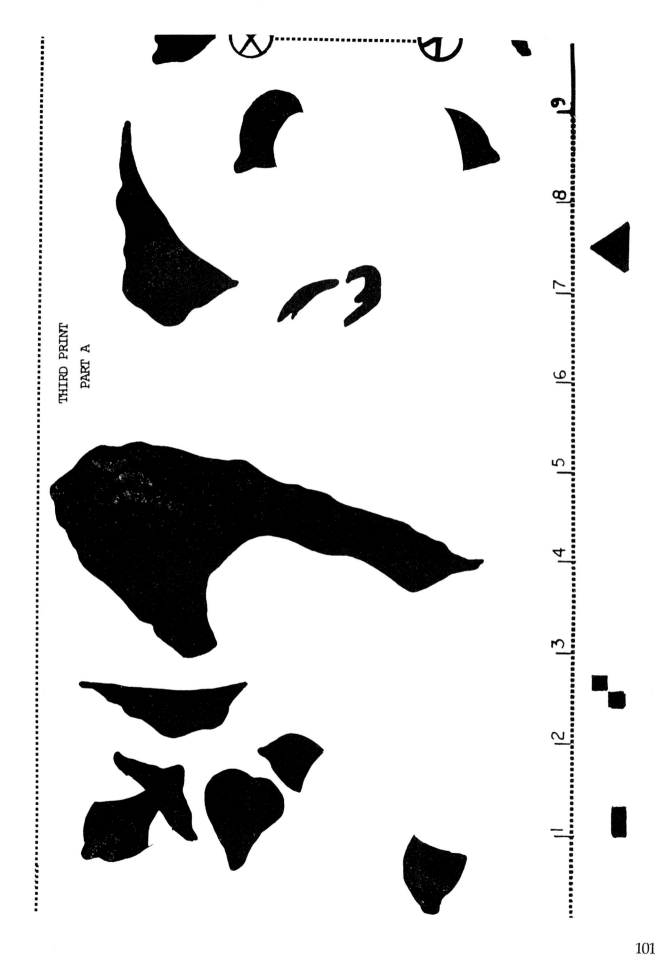

THIRD PRINT
PART A

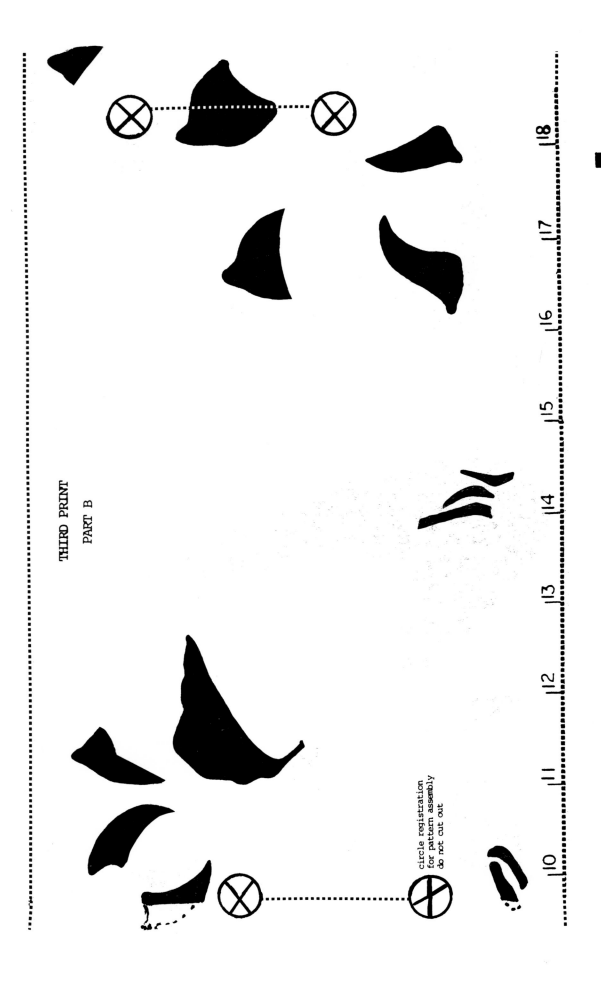

THIRD PRINT

PART B

circle registration
for pattern assembly
do not cut out

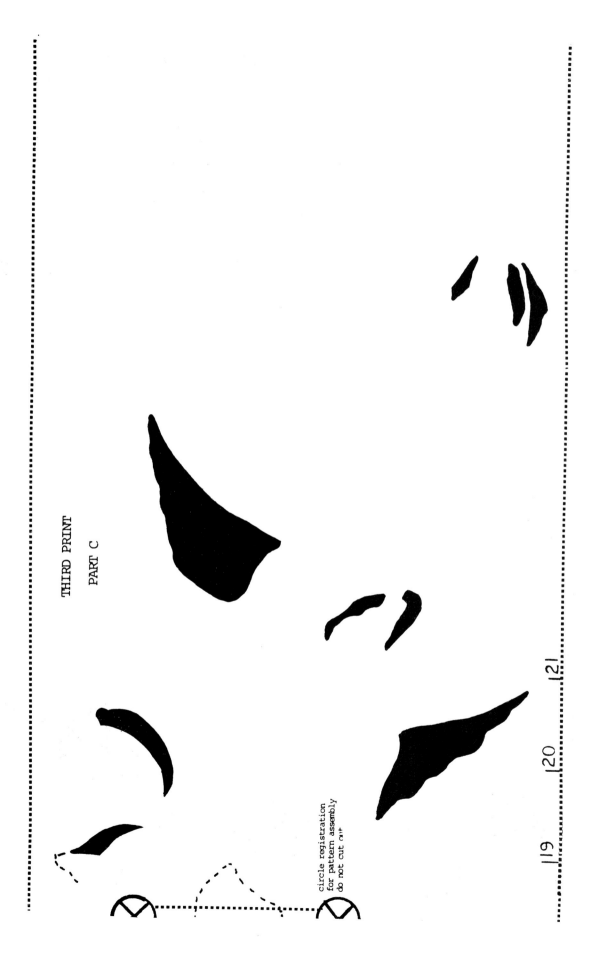

THIRD PRINT

PART C

circle registration
for pattern assembly
do not cut out

|19

|20

|21

103

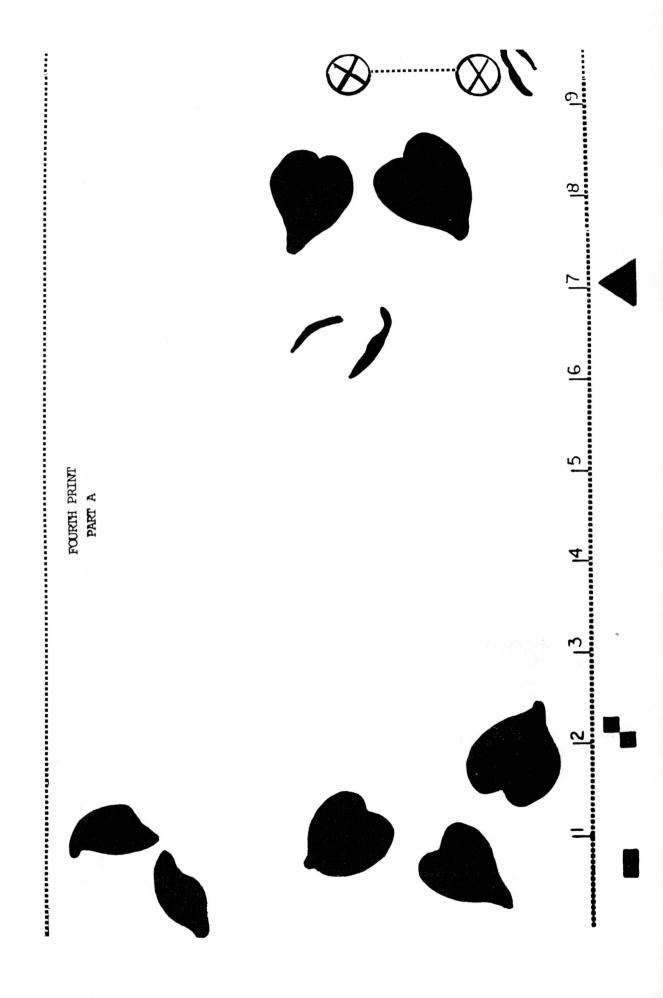

FOURTH PRINT
PART A

104

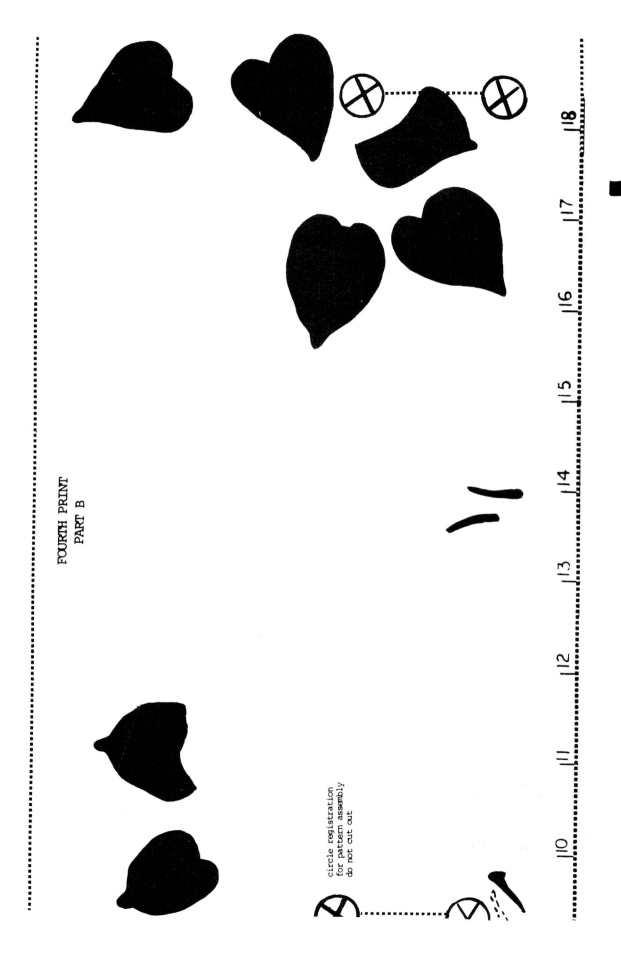

FOURTH PRINT
PART B

circle registration
for pattern assembly
do not cut out

10   11   12   13   14   15   16   17   18

105

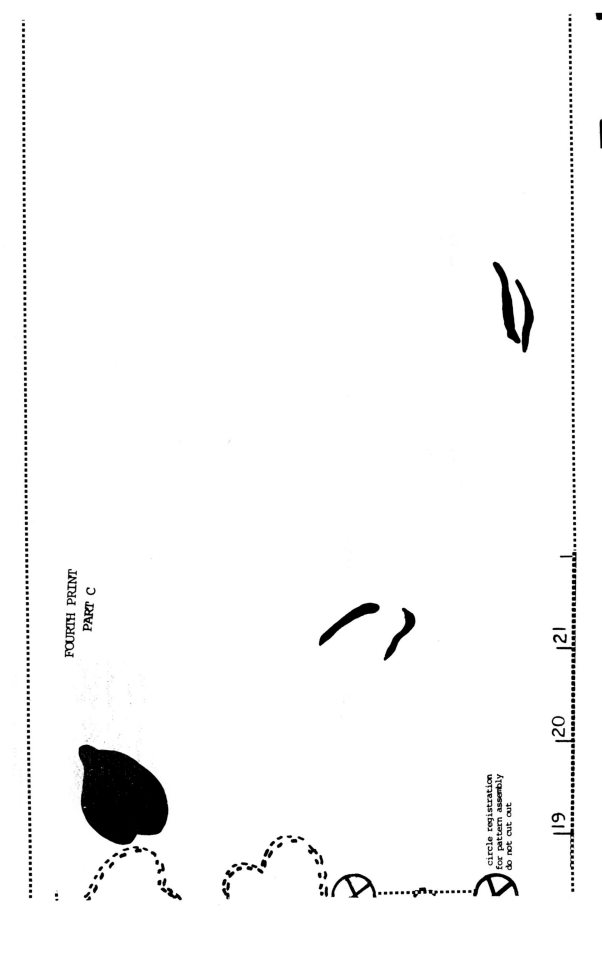

FOURTH PRINT
PART C

circle registration
for pattern assembly
do not cut out

19   20   21

CALIFORNIA POPPY

The poppy border, based on the state wildflower of California, looks great against a background as blue as the state's famous skies. In addition, try underlining it with the split-squares miniborder.

HEIGHT:

11 inches

NUMBER OF TEMPLATES:

Four

TIME:

2 hours to transfer and cut; 10 minutes to print 3 feet with complete design.

SIZING TO FIT ROOM:

The design has been drawn to repeat at 10 inches; it can be expanded to 10½ inches. Random element—a sprig of poppy leaves—can be inserted where needed to fill gaps. Random element is 3½ inches wide.

COLORS

Use acrylics unless noted otherwise.

Hooker's Green	Raw Umber
Cerulean Blue	Yellow Oxide/Yellow Ochre
Yellow Orange AZO	White latex
Red Orange Indo	

BRUSHES:

Two No. 10 stencil brushes (one for greens and one for oranges).

PRINTING:

Print 1—Poppy stems are printed on the baseline in grey-green mixed from Hooker's Green, Cerulean Blue, Raw Umber and white. Vary the lightness of paint slightly from stem to stem if you wish.

Print 2—Add white and yellow to the poppy stem color used for print 1 to print second stem group. These stems will be lighter and more yellow, but still grey-green.

Print 3—Poppy petals are pure Yellow Orange AZO. If printed over darker background, print undercoat of white before applying orange, since it is a transparent color.

Print 4—Print the rest of the poppy petals in reddish orange mixed from Red Orange Indo and Yellow Orange AZO. As with the first set of poppy petals, if printing on a dark background, apply an undercoat of white before printing petal color.

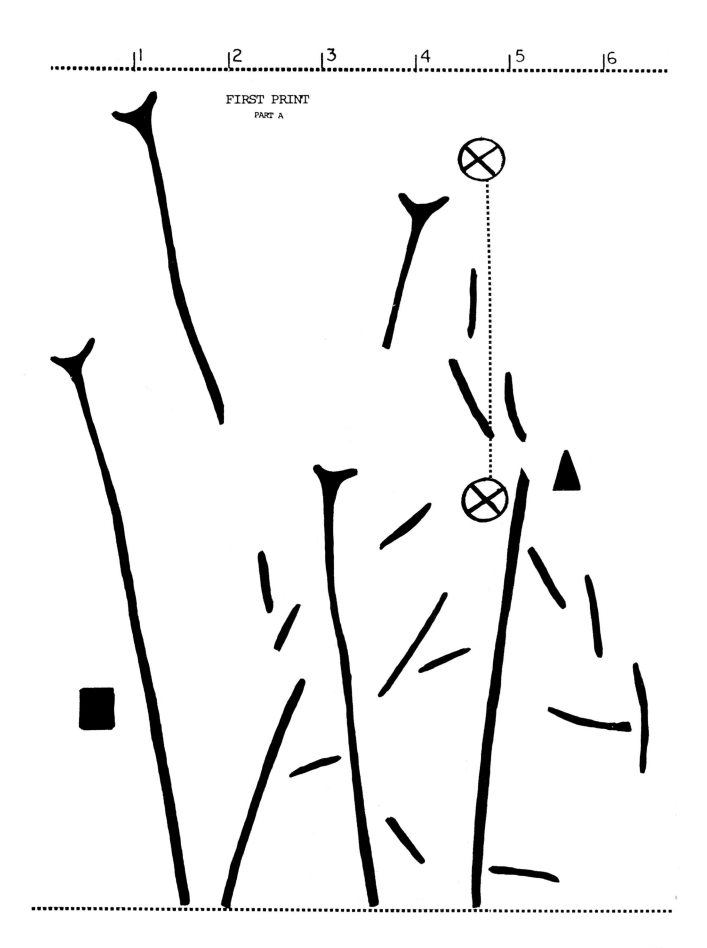

FIRST PRINT
PART A

109

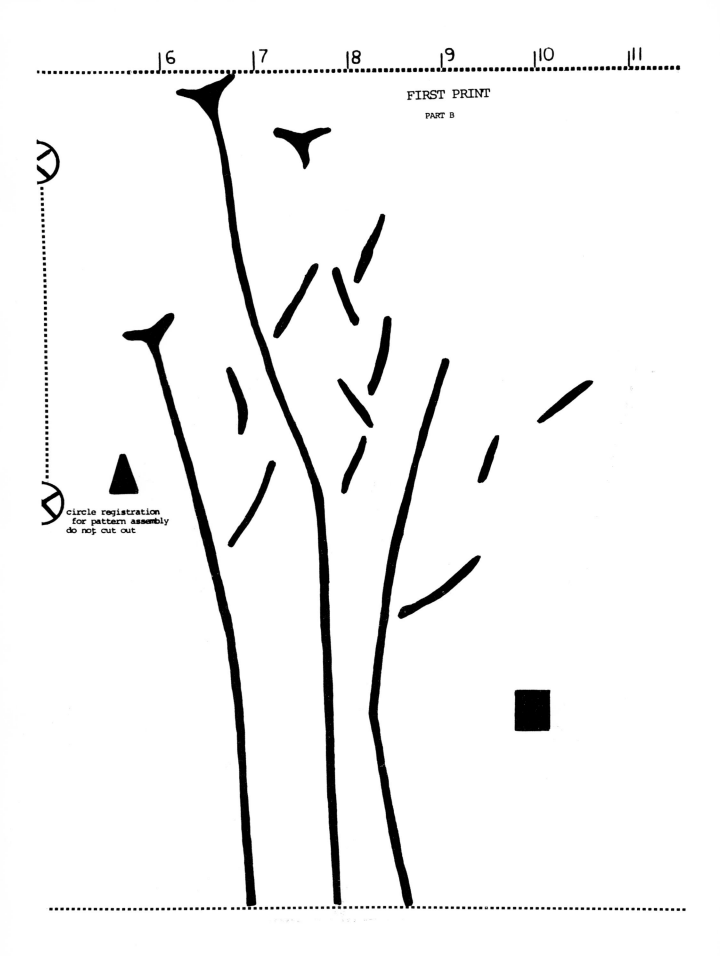

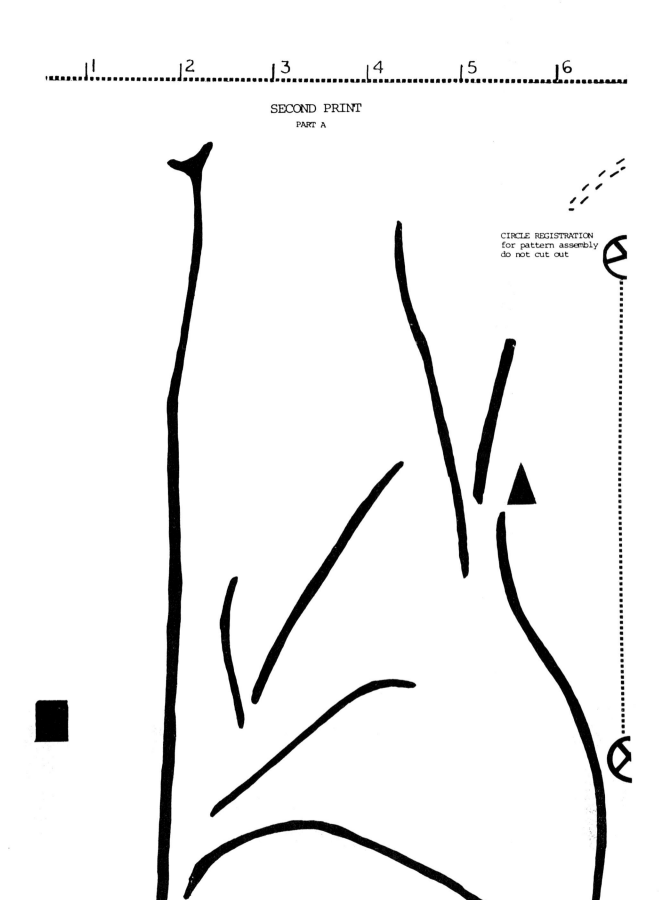

SECOND PRINT
PART A

CIRCLE REGISTRATION
for pattern assembly
do not cut out

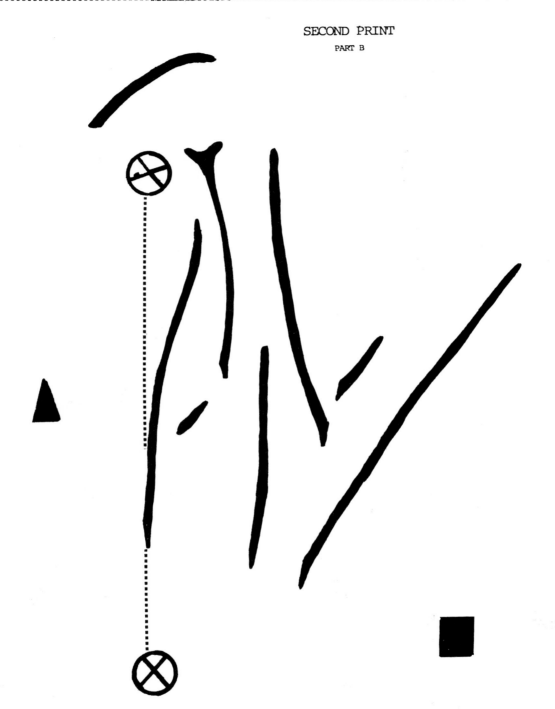

SECOND PRINT
PART B

THIRD PRINT

PART A

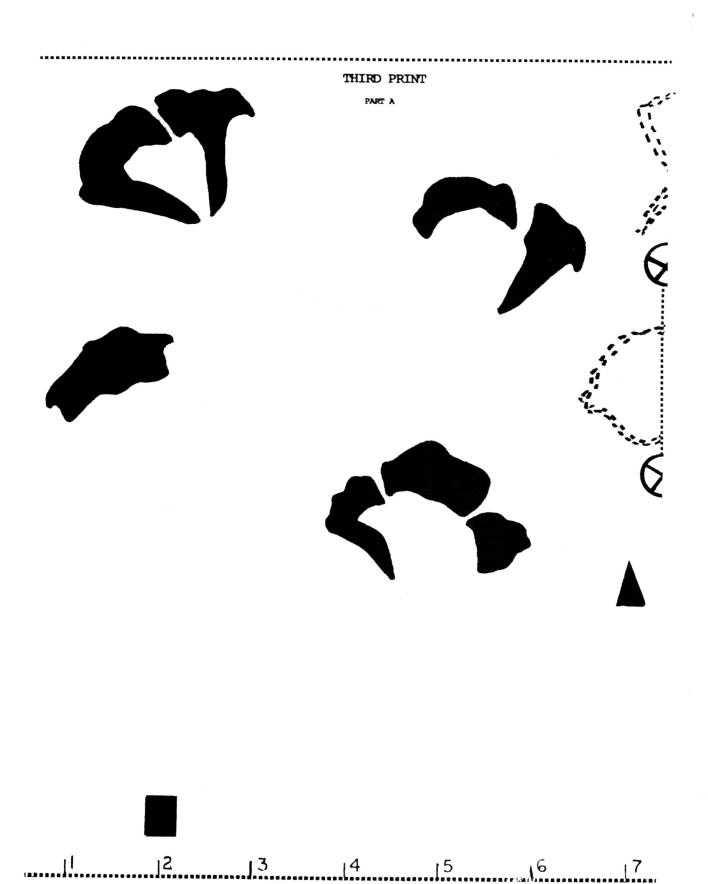

THIRD PRINT

PART B

circle registration
for pattern assembly
do not cut out

|7 |8 |9 |10 |11 |12 |

114

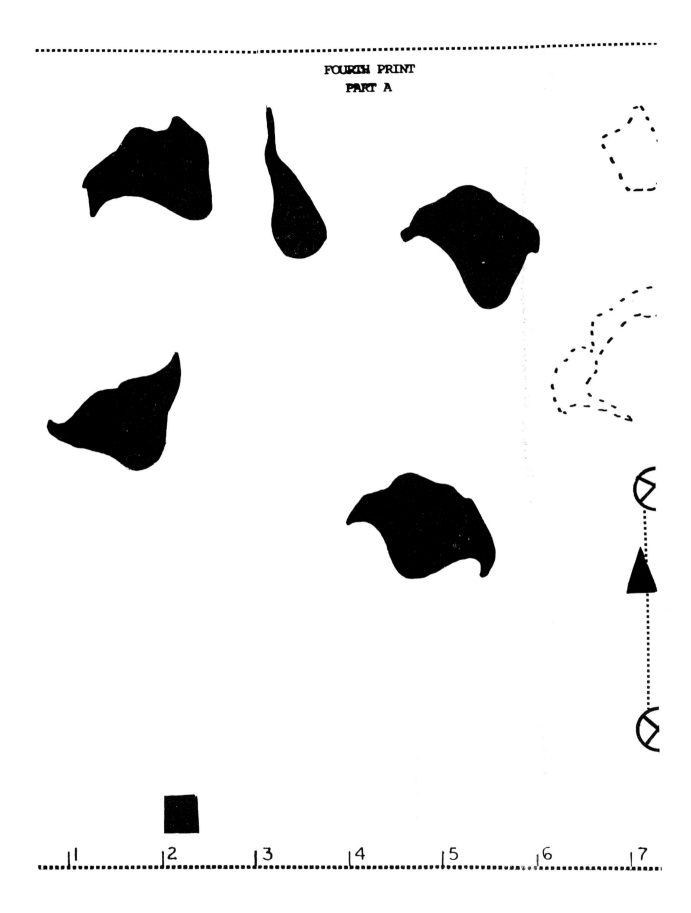

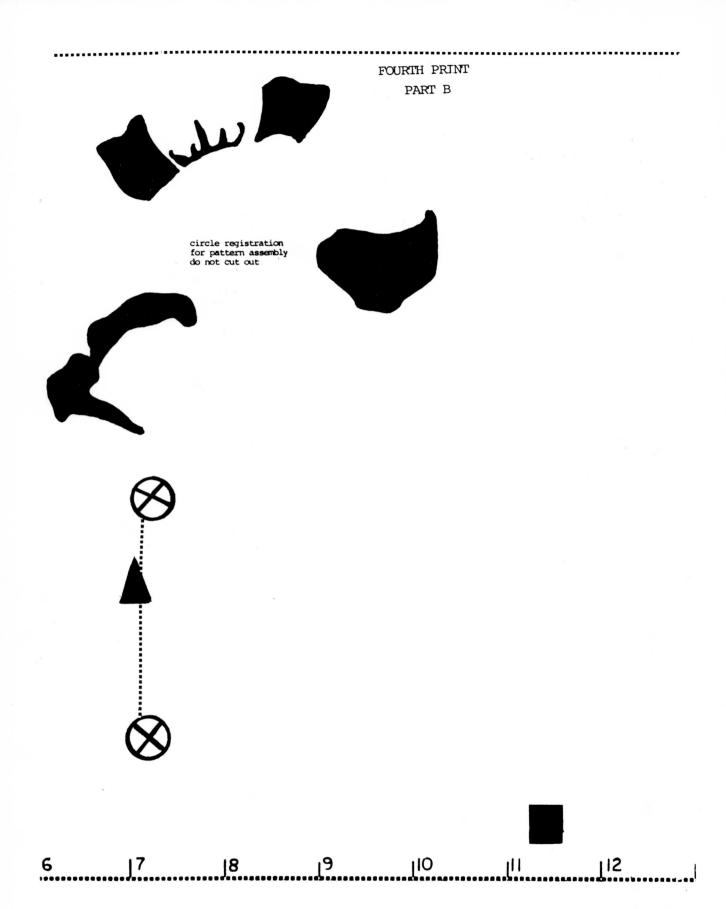

FOURTH PRINT
PART B

circle registration
for pattern assembly
do not cut out

6 |7 |8 |9 |10 |11 |12

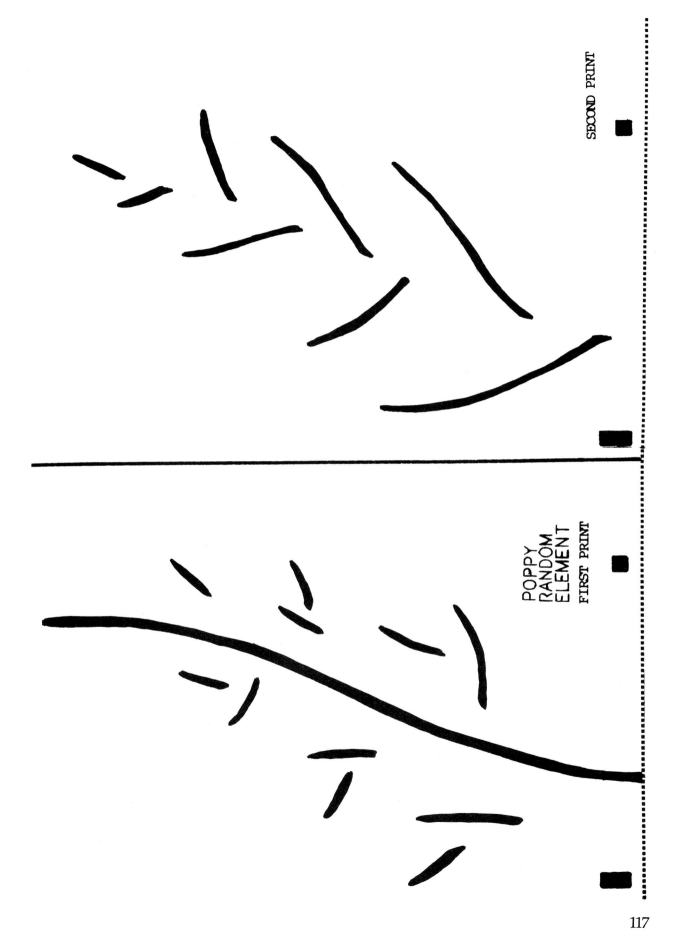

POPPY
RANDOM
ELEMENT
FIRST PRINT

SECOND PRINT

117

NASTURTIUM

COMMENTS:

The nasturtium border has been designed to resemble Art Deco stained glass. It is printed on a background stripe of a brownish red or other dark color.

HEIGHT:

6⅛ inches

NUMBER OF TEMPLATES:

Four large, three small

TIME:

3½ hours to transfer and cut; 20 minutes to print a 3-foot section with complete image.

SIZING TO FIT ROOM:

Pattern repeats every 13¾ inches. It cannot be expanded. To gracefully cover the seam where the border meets itself, stencil a small 3¼-inch block—it looks like a tile with a nasturtium on it. If there are natural breaks in the border, such as where it meets a window, you can end the border on either side of the opening. Then you won't need to print the block. If you like the block, you can use it at set intervals all around the room.

COLORS

Use acrylics unless noted otherwise.

Hooker's Green	Cadmium Red, Medium
Brilliant Yellow	Ultramarine Blue
Raw Umber	Thalo Blue
Yellow Orange AZO	White latex

(Background stripe was painted in reddish brown with latex house paint).

BRUSHES:

At least two and preferably four No. 10 stencil brushes.

PRINTING:

Background stripe. Paint a background stripe 6⅛ inches wide in red-brown or other dark color, following instructions in To Lay a Background Stripe section.

Print 1—Yellow-green for leaves is a mixture of Hooker's Green and Brilliant Yellow with small amounts of white latex and Raw Umber.

Print 2—Color the second group of leaves darker than the first, using the same stencil brush and the same color formula but with less white and yellow.

Print 3—First print all flower shapes with an undercoat of white. Leaving the template in place, let the white dry. Then print flowers in a variety of colors—one color to a flower. Use Yellow Orange AZO, Brilliant Yellow and Cadmium Red, Medium. Paint the middles of Brilliant Yellow flowers with a pounce of Yellow Orange AZO.

Print 4—Paint the top half blue, using a mixture of Ultramarine Blue, Raw Umber, Thalo Blue, and white latex. Paint the bottom half dark green by mixing Hooker's Green, Ultramarine Blue, and Raw Umber. You can apply with the same stencil brush as the one used for print 1 without washing.

Block—The block is printed from three small templates in the same manner and colors as the larger nasturtium pattern: first print (leaves and outside edge), green; second print (flowers) same as flowers in border; third print (background) all blue.

Since the block prints in the same colors as the large border, it is easiest to print both at the same time. If you decide to use the block at frequent intervals, mask off those areas with a shield of thick paper that is 3¼ inches wide by 7 inches long. Use masking tape to attach the shield to the wall by its top corners. Print the large border right over the shield. Then flip the shield up to print the block. Flip the shield back down to print the next template for the border. Then flip it up again to print the corresponding small template for the block.

Remember to put a block where the border seams.

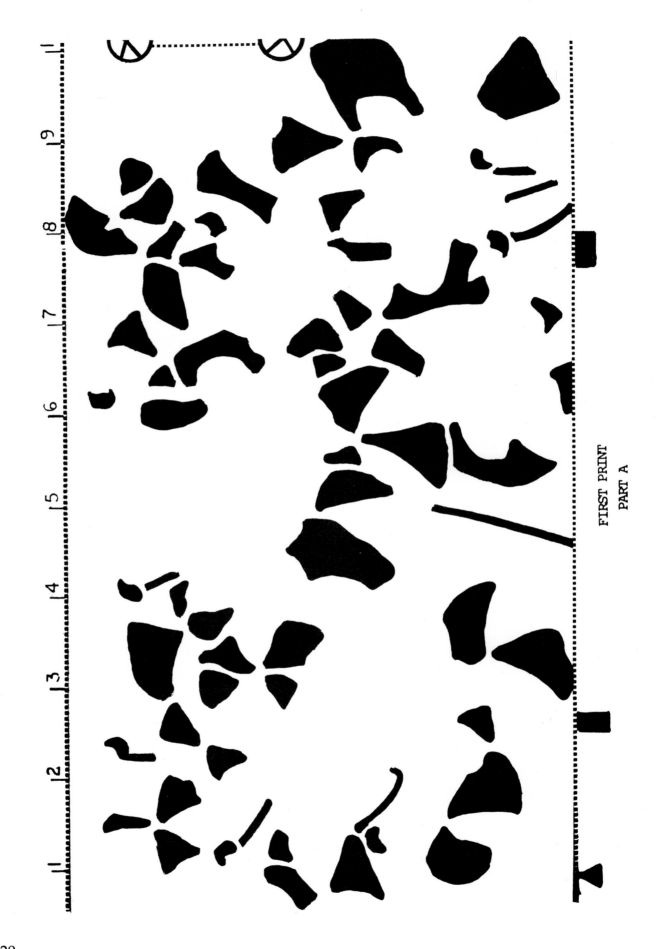

FIRST PRINT
PART A

120

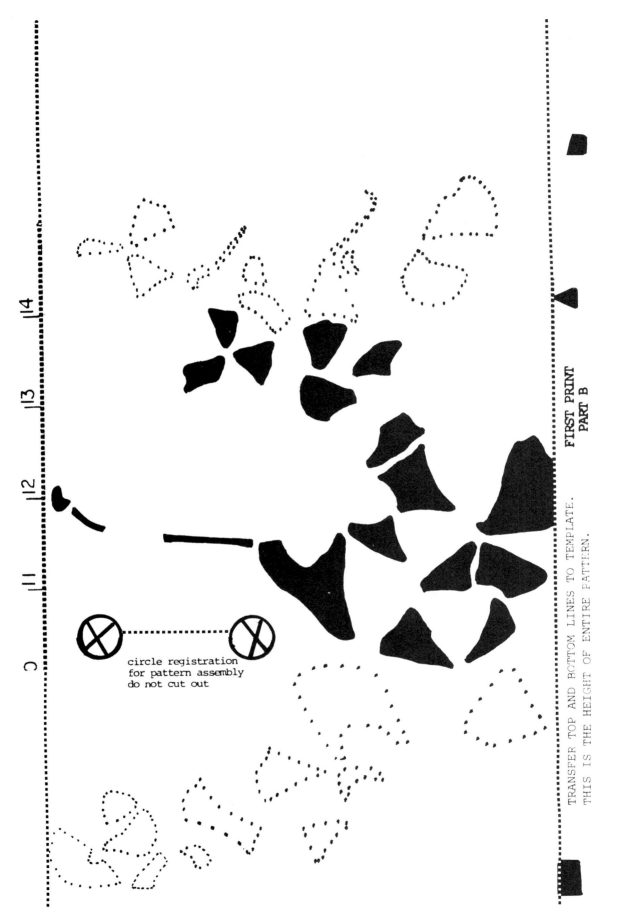

C   11   12   13   14

circle registration
for pattern assembly
do not cut out

FIRST PRINT
PART B

TRANSFER TOP AND BOTTOM LINES TO TEMPLATE.
THIS IS THE HEIGHT OF ENTIRE PATTERN.

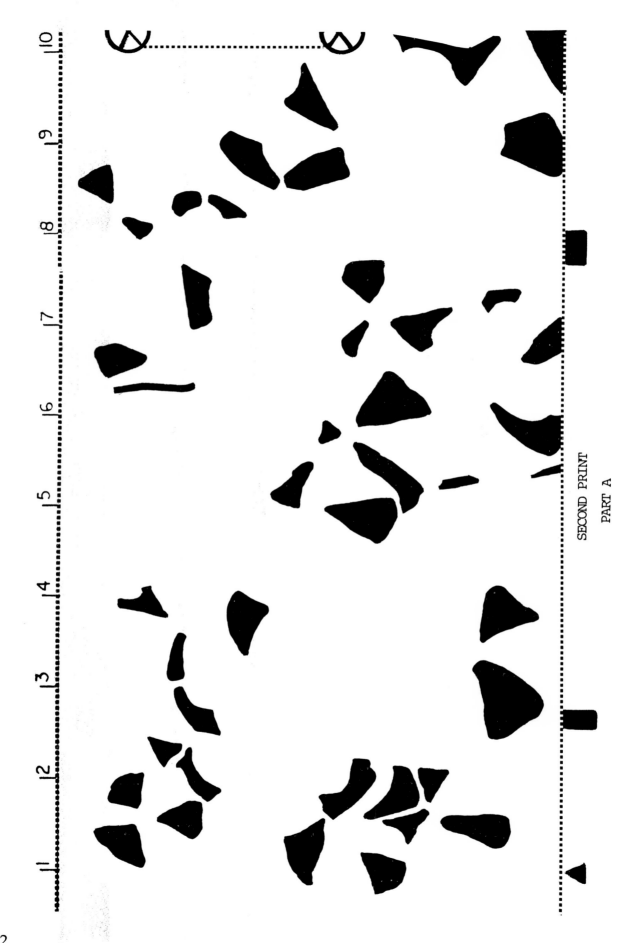

SECOND PRINT

PART A

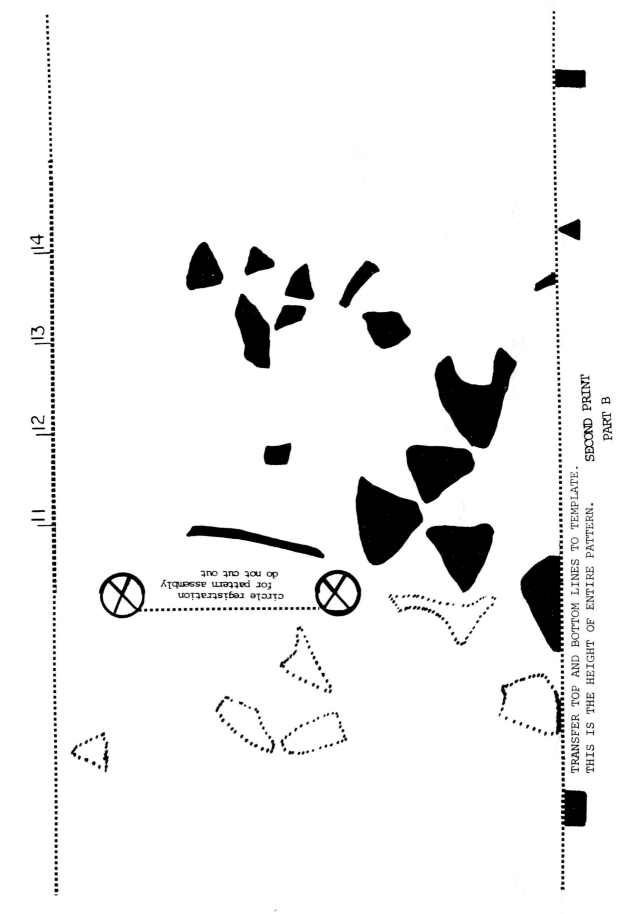

TRANSFER TOP AND BOTTOM LINES TO TEMPLATE.
THIS IS THE HEIGHT OF ENTIRE PATTERN.

SECOND PRINT
PART B

circle registration
for pattern assembly
do not cut out

123

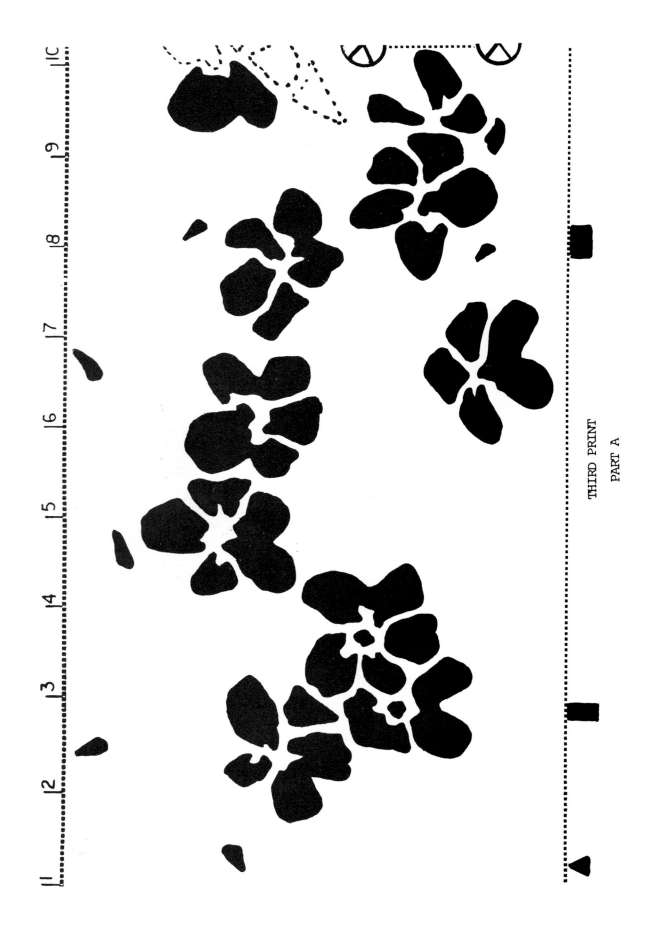

THIRD PRINT
PART A

124

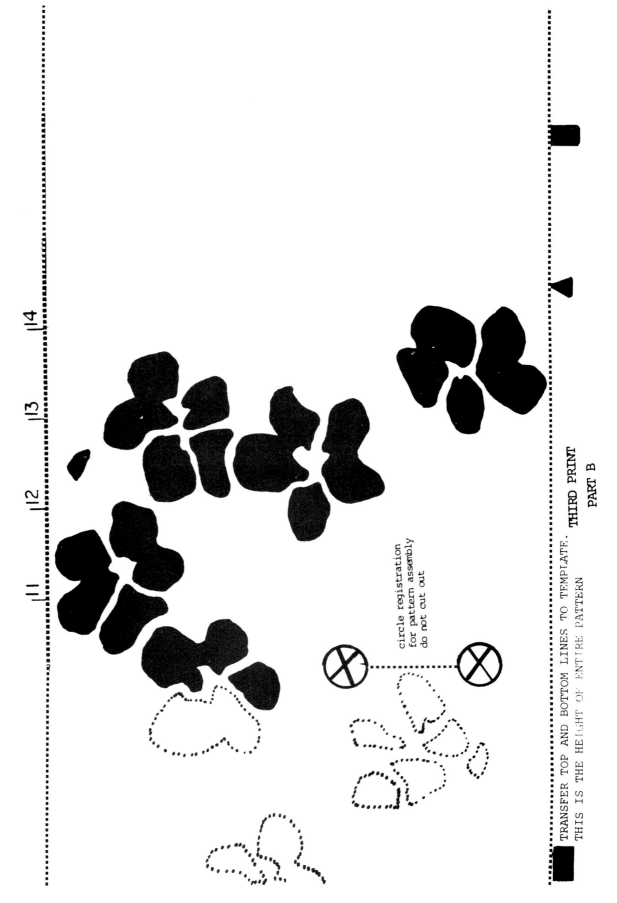

circle registration
for pattern assembly
do not cut out

TRANSFER TOP AND BOTTOM LINES TO TEMPLATE. **THIRD PRINT**
THIS IS THE HEIGHT OF ENTIRE PATTERN   PART B

125

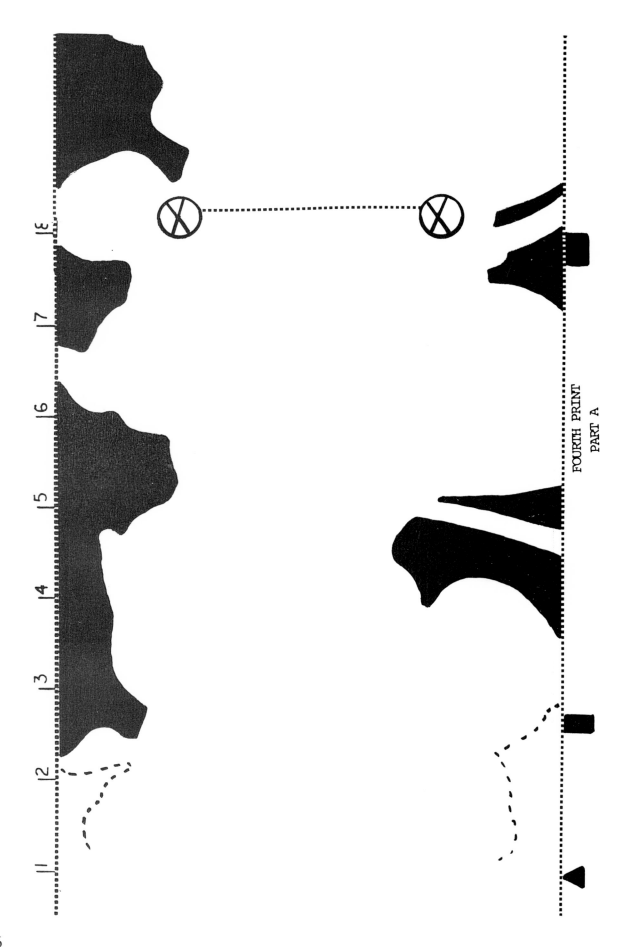

FOURTH PRINT
PART A

126

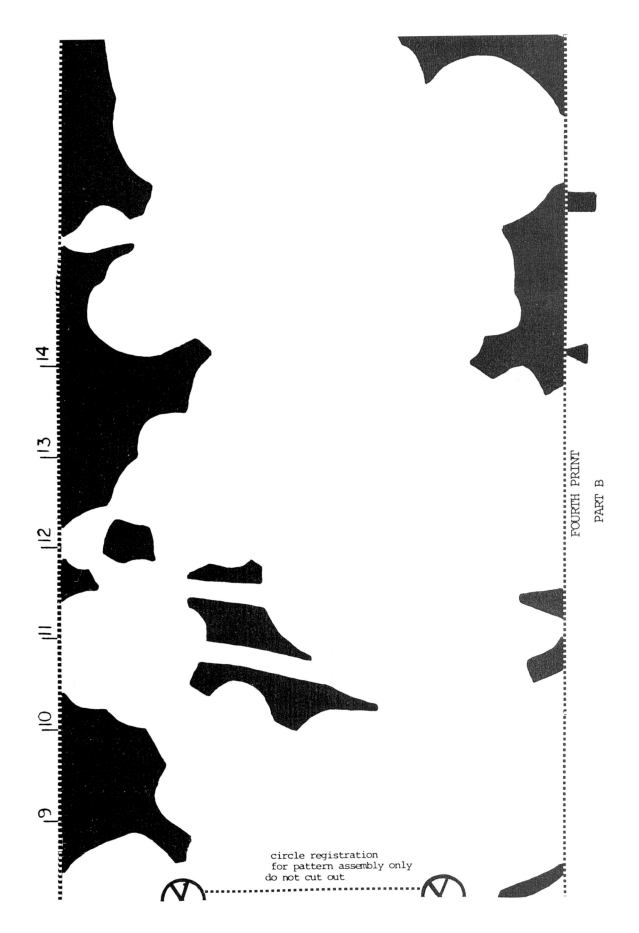

9   10   11   12   13   14

FOURTH PRINT

PART B

circle registration
for pattern assembly only
do not cut out

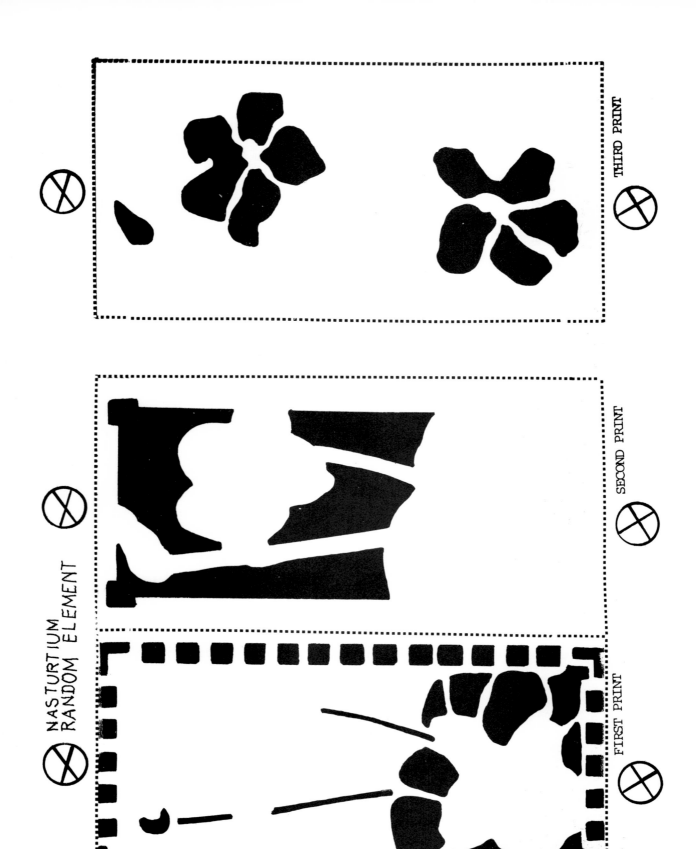

NASTURTIUM
RANDOM ELEMENT

FIRST PRINT

SECOND PRINT

THIRD PRINT

128

ROSE

Large and elegant upon the wall, the free-flowing rose border is not as difficult as it appears. The hardest part is cutting out the delicate shapes.

HEIGHT:

13¼ inches

NUMBER OF TEMPLATES:

Four

TIME:

4½ hours to transfer and cut; 25 minutes to print 3 feet with the entire design.

SIZING TO FIT ROOM:

As drawn, rose repeats at 12½ inches. It can be expanded to 13½ inches.

COLORS

Use acrylic paints unless noted otherwise.

Hooker's Green   Quinacridone Violet/Acra Violet
Cadmium Yellow, Light   Raw Umber
Naphthol Crimson   White latex
Ultramarine Blue

BRUSHES:

Three No. 10 stencil brushes.

PRINTING:

Print 1—The leaf color is a mixture of Hooker's Green with Raw Umber and small amount of white.

Print 2—Parts of the leaves you just painted will be visible through cutouts. Overpaint these a dark blue-green that is mixed from Hooker's Green, Ultramarine Blue, and a few drops of white. Print the other cutouts (through which only blank wall can be seen) with very light yellow-green that is mixed from Cadmium Yellow, Light, Hooker's Green, and white (Illus. 42–43).

Illus. 42. To decide which areas of print 2 get printed with dark green, look in openings of template. If you see green, then they get overprinted with the dark green for shading.

Illus. 43. Completed second print showing two-tone shading of leaves and light color stems.

Print 3—First print the entire template in light yellow made by mixing Cadmium Yellow, Light with white. Leave the template in place. Mix a pink from Naphthol Crimson and white with a small amount of Quinacridone Violet. Load the brush with pink, and then pounce on paper towels until brush is almost dry and begins to paint speckles. Softly swirl the brush against the edges of the cutouts to make them pink blending into yellow (Illus. 44). See Special Effects for additional instructions.

Illus. 44. Finished third print showing shading of rose blossom. Note the soft blending that a dry brush gives.

Print 4—Use a slightly darker shade of the pink mixed with a small amount of yellow to print shading details for roses (Illus. 45).

OTHER IDEAS:

Make red roses or all-yellow roses. Whatever color you use, the rose details (print 4) must be darker than the rose. For yellow rose, use deep yellow details; for red roses, burgundy.

Illus. 45. Fourth print of rose is petal shadows. Note registration alignment.

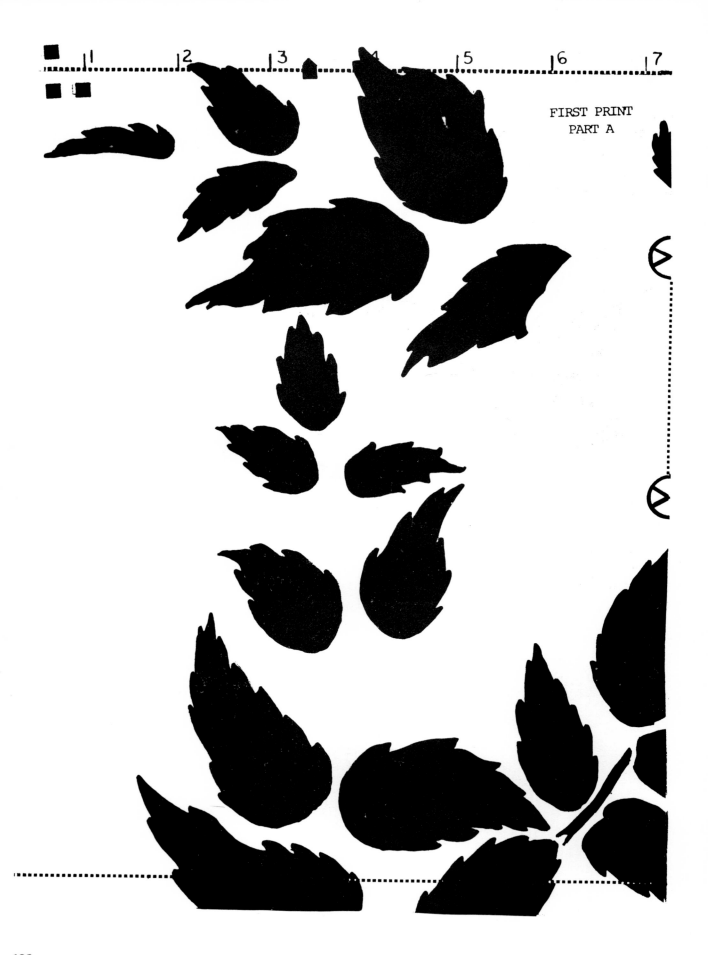

FIRST PRINT
PART A

FIRST PRINT
PART B

circle registration
for pattern assembly
do not cut out

133

SECOND PRINT
PART A

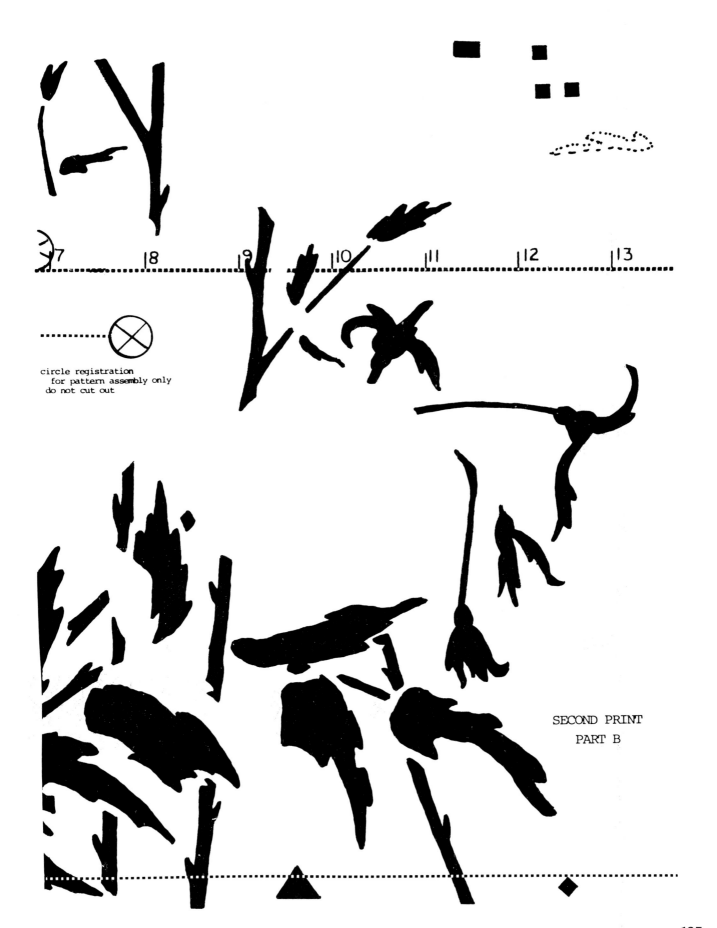

circle registration
for pattern assembly only
do not cut out

7   8   9   10   11   12   13

SECOND PRINT
PART B

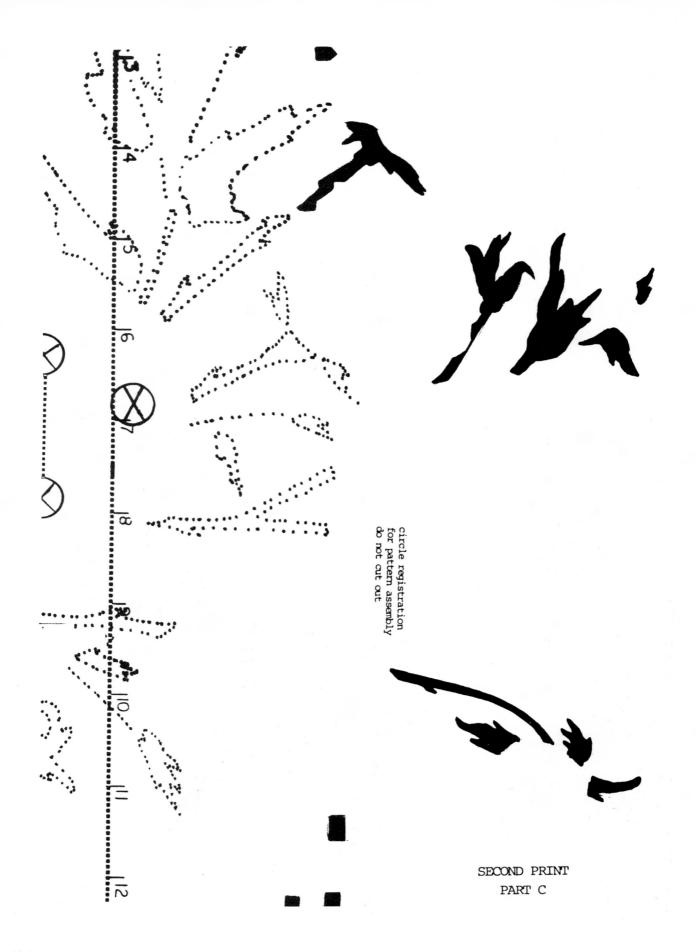

circle registration
for pattern assembly
do not cut out

SECOND PRINT
PART C

THIRD PRINT

PART A

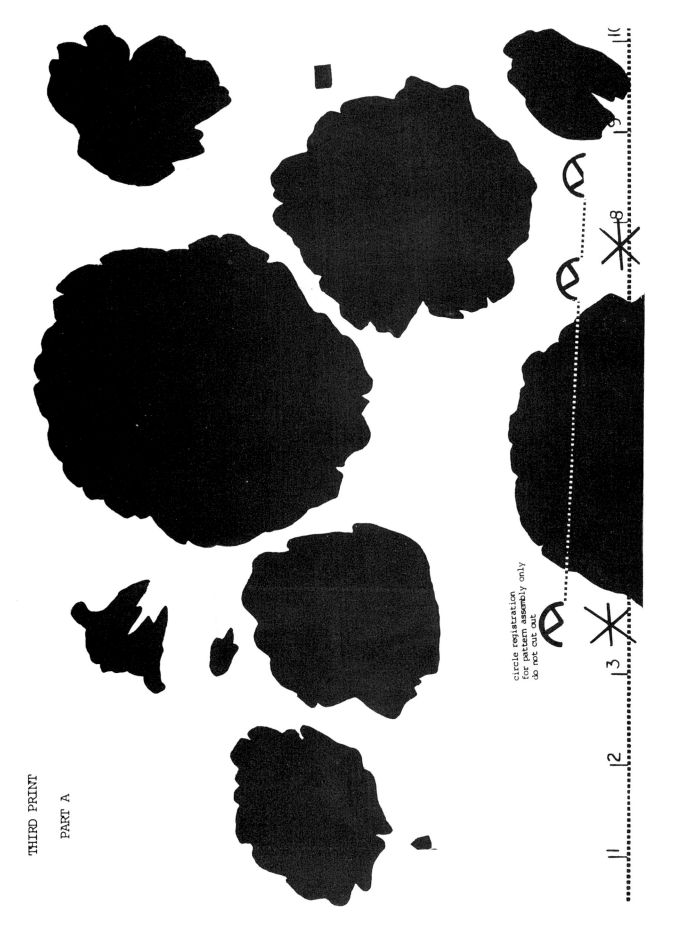

circle registration
for pattern assembly only
do not cut out

THIRD PRINT
PART B

DAFFODIL

Copy the colors of your favorite daffodil or narcissus for this border. You can even have lime-green daffodils. The daffodils look billowy printed on a sky-blue background stripe or more tailored underlined with a miniborder of split squares.

HEIGHT:

9⅞ inches

NUMBER OF TEMPLATES:

Four

TIME:

2½ hours to transfer and cut; 15 minutes to print 3-foot section with complete image.

SIZING TO FIT ROOM:

As drawn, design repeats at 12 inches. It can be expanded to 12½ inches. Fill additional gaps by printing the daffodil on the right-hand side by itself as a random element. It takes up 2½ to 3 inches. Registration marks—a square above a rectangle to the left of the blossom and a large square to the right—help align and print the random blossom.

COLORS

Use acrylics unless noted otherwise.

Chromium Oxide Green	Red Oxide
Brilliant Yellow	Yellow Oxide/Yellow Ochre
Ultramarine Blue	White latex
Yellow Orange AZO	

(Yellow Orange AZO and Red Oxide are necessary only if you wish to print the trumpets in a contrasting color. The print in Illus. 46 shows three-color, two-color and all-yellow daffodils. Instructions are given for two-tone and all-yellow daffodils).

BRUSHES:

Two No. 10 and one No. 2 stencil brushes for yellow daffodils with details on petals. Another No. 2 stencil brush is needed for two-tone daffodils.

PRINTING:

Print 1—Leaves and stems in yellow-green mixed from Chromium Oxide Green and Brilliant Yellow. Apply with No. 10 brush.

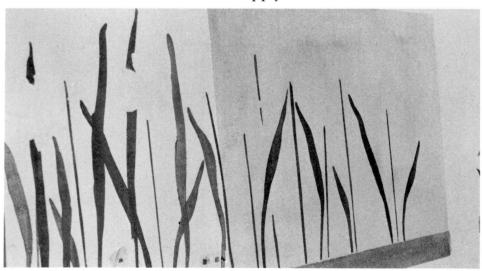

Illus. 46. On the left are daffodil prints 1 and 2 with registration marks in place. On the right on background stripe is print one only. Notice how close the print shapes are to the registration marks; so keep those tape pieces small.

Print 2—Leaves—some blue-green and some yellow-green. Mix blue-green from Ultramarine Blue, Chromium Oxide Green and white; for yellow-green combine Chromium Oxide Green, Brilliant Yellow, and white. Use the same No. 10 stencil brush used for print 1.

Print 3—Print flower shapes Brilliant Yellow. If background is not white, apply an undercoat of white before printing with yellow. (For white flowers, two coats of white.) Use a No. 10 stencil brush.

Optional print 3—For two-tone daffodils, print trumpets in Yellow Orange AZO mixed with a small amount of Yellow Ochre. Use No. 10 stencil brush used for print 2. Skip this step for one-color daffodils.

Print 4—The shading details for the daffodils are printed in a darker shade than the flower color. For all-yellow daffodils, print details in Yellow Oxide. For yellow daffodils with orange trumpets, print petal details with Yellow Oxide and middle of trumpet very lightly with Red Oxide mixed with Yellow Orange AZO. Use No. 2 stencil brush.

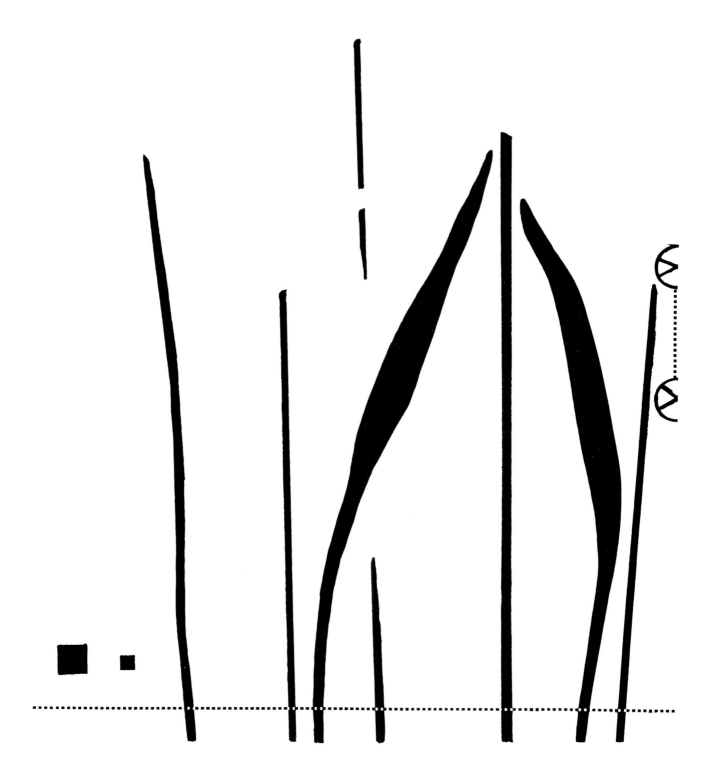

FIRST PRINT

PART A

143

FIRST PRINT

PART B

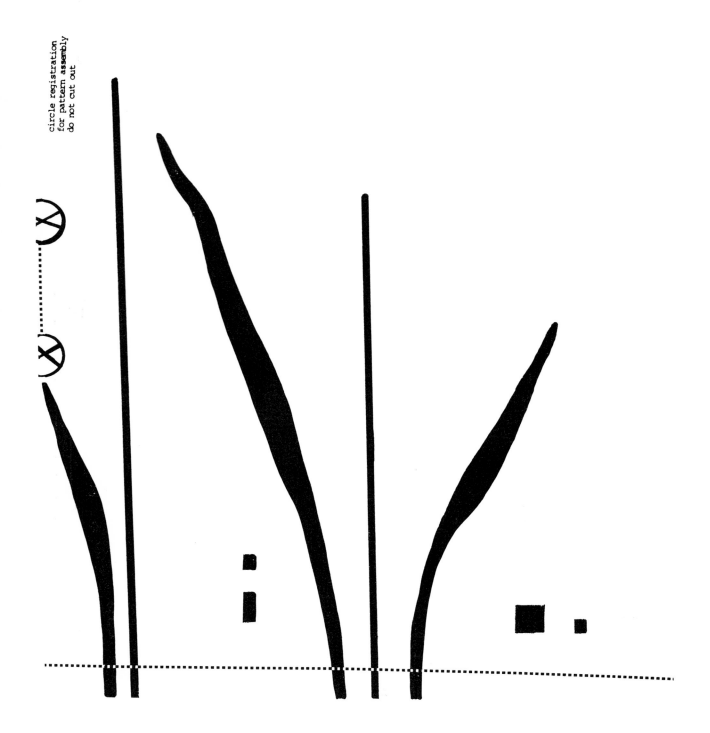

circle registration
for pattern assembly
do not cut out

SECOND PRINT
PART A

145

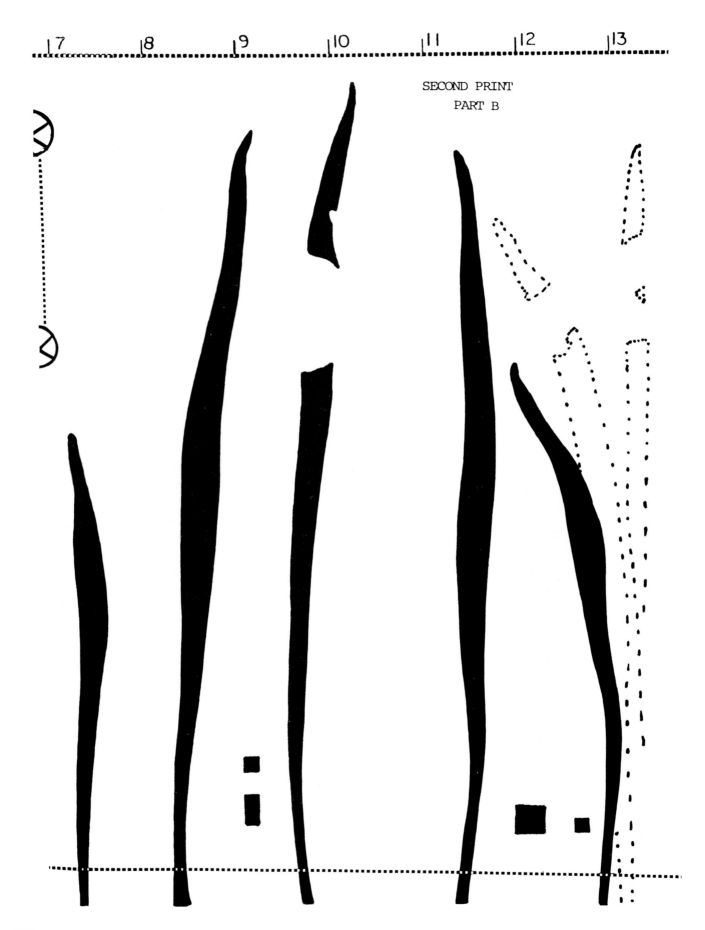

SECOND PRINT
PART B

146

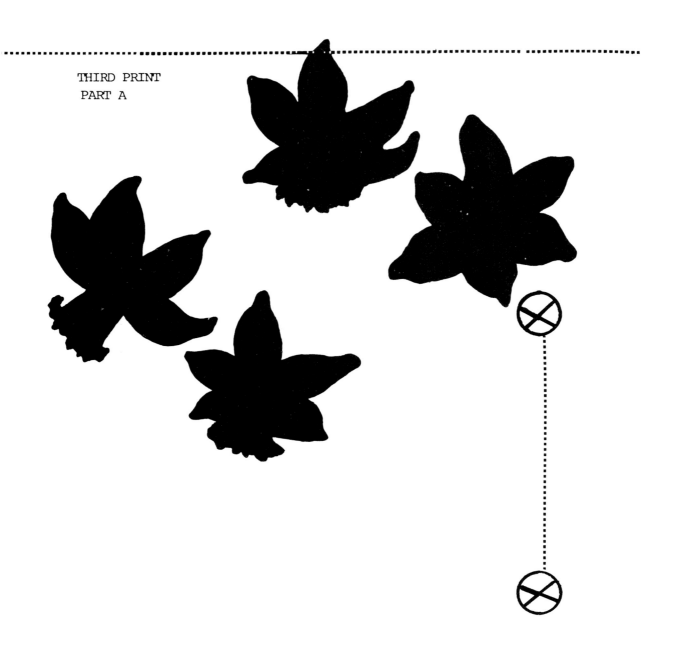

THIRD PRINT
PART A

THIS IS THE BASELINE. TRANSFER TO TEMPLATE.

circle registration
for pattern assembly
do not cut out

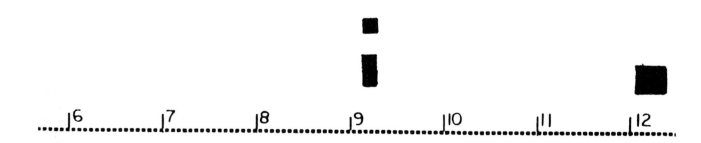

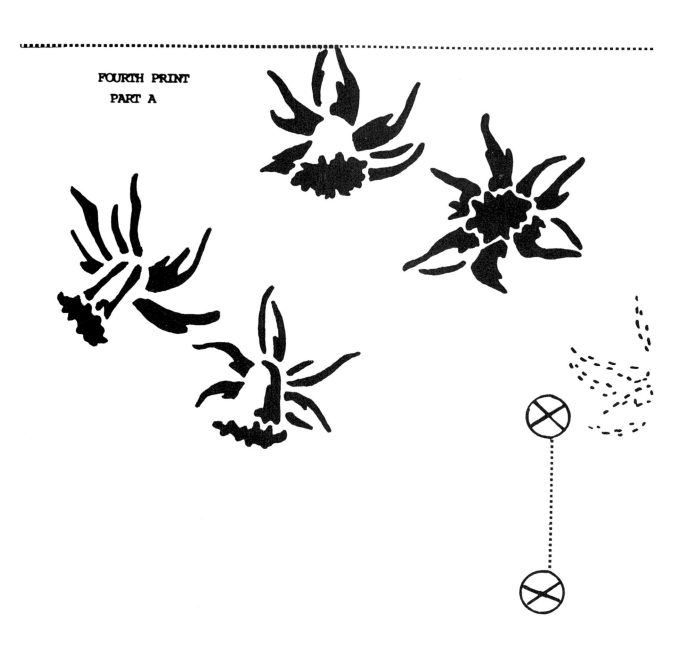

FOURTH PRINT
PART A

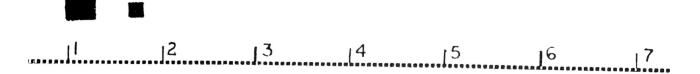

circle registration
for pattern assembly
do not cut out

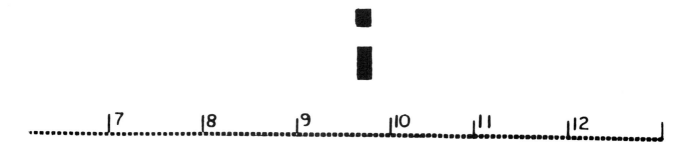

**PRINT
PART A**

PRINT

PART B

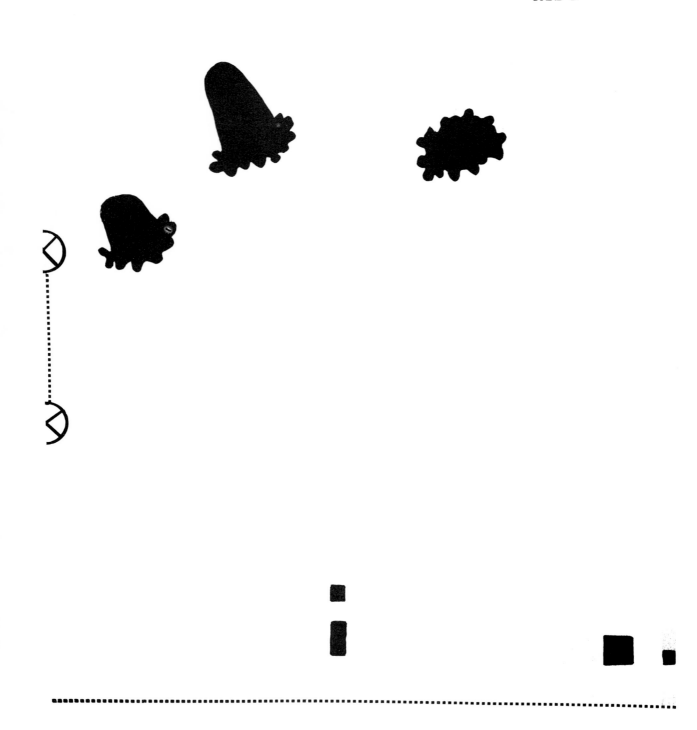

Miscellaneous Borders and Patterns

ART DECO

The Art Deco miniborder of one template looks like a plaster moulding or an engraved design. It can be printed with either edge up. Printing will go faster if you cut a double length of the border. For fancy effect, double-print the border over the same path. First print it with triangles up, then reprint it with triangles down and moved over a bit so they fall between the motif already printed.

HEIGHT:
1½ inches

REPEAT:
1½ inches

BRUSHES:
One No. 10 stencil brush.

PRINTING:
Register by matching end of design on template over last motif on wall.

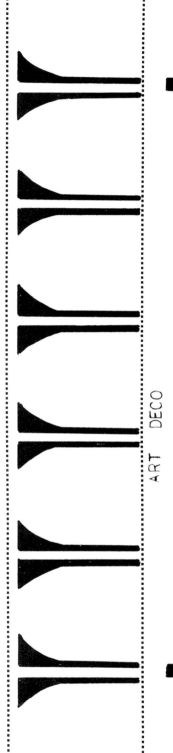

ART DECO

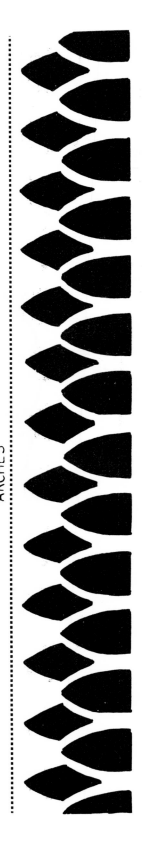

ARCHED BORDER

The one-template arched border looks good with arches pointed down as crown border or, with arches pointed up, underneath the fern. Transfer and cut two lengths of design for speedier printing.

HEIGHT:

1⅜ inches

REPEAT:

¾ inch

TIME:

20 minutes to cut and transfer; 4 minutes to print 3 feet.

REPEAT:

Every ¾ inch. Register by fitting the last open space on the stencil over the last of the arches already printed.

COLORS:

Looks good in any color and is especially attractive mounted on lighter or darker background stripe.

BRUSHES:

One No. 10 stencil brush.

PRINTING:

If you are printing over a background stripe for a fancy effect, draw the position of the background stripe on top of the template. Then align these lines with the background stripe as you print. For another effect, print arches shaded in two colors, such as green coming down from the top, blue coming up from the bottom.

SPLIT SQUARES

Transfer and cut two lengths of the design onto the template, because it prints much faster in longer sections. This is a one-template design.

HEIGHT:
⅝ inch

TIME:
40 minutes to transfer and cut; 2 minutes to print 3 feet.

REPEAT:
¾ inch

BRUSHES:
One No. 10 stencil brush.

PRINTING:
Register by fitting end of template over last motif printed (Illus. 47).

SQUARES MINI-BORDER

Illus. 47. All miniborders are registered off the last shape printed. They also have the background stripe width marked on the template to allow centering of template on stripe.

162

INDEX